The Girls' World Book of
FRIENDSHIP CRAFTS
cool stuff to make with your best friends

Joanne O'Sullivan

LARK BOOKS

A Division of Sterling Publishing Co., Inc.
New York

Assistant Editor: Nathalie Mornu
Senior Editor: Paige Gilchrist
Art Director: Tom Metcalf
Photographer: Sandra Stambaugh
Cover Designer: Barbara Zaretsky
Illustrator: August Hoerr
Associate Art Director: Shannon Yokeley
Editorial Assistance: Delores Gosnell, Rosemary Kast, Jeff Hamilton
Editorial Interns: Amanda Wheeler, Meghan McGuire

10 9 8 7 6 5 4 3 2 1

First Edition

Published by Lark Books, A Division of
Sterling Publishing Co., Inc.
387 Park Avenue South, New York, N.Y. 10016

© 2005, Lark Books

Distributed in Canada by Sterling Publishing,
c/o Canadian Manda Group, 165 Dufferin Street
Toronto, Ontario, Canada M6K 3H6

Distributed in the U.K. by Guild of Master Craftsman Publications Ltd., Castle Place, 166 High Street, Lewes, East Sussex, England
BN7 1XU
Tel: (+ 44) 1273 477374, Fax: (+ 44) 1273 478606, Email: pubs@thegmcgroup.com, Web: www.gmcpublications.com

Distributed in Australia by Capricorn Link (Australia) Pty Ltd.,
P.O. Box 704, Windsor, NSW 2756 Australia

If you have questions or comments about this book, please contact:
Lark Books
67 Broadway
Asheville, NC 28801
(828) 253-0467

Manufactured in China

ISBN 1-57990-471-8

Introduction

They're always there when you need them and they never let you down. They keep your secrets, and lift your spirits when you're feeling blue. Your best friends deserve the best of everything, so we've come up with more than 50 of the best projects you'll ever find to make for and with your friends.

The best gifts come from the heart, not from a store. For cool gift ideas just right for your friends, turn to the Best Gifts section of the book. These are not your run-of-the-mill, came-from-the-mall type of gifts. Your friends are special and your gifts to them can be, too. Choose one of the many easy project ideas that anyone can do, no experience necessary, or get an adult to help you with a project that requires a little more skill. There are gift ideas for every kind of girl, so you're sure to find one that's perfect for every friend. When you're done making your gift, add a card or special wrapping to it using the ideas at the end of the chapter.

In the Best Memories section of the book, you'll find project ideas that celebrate your friendship and help you and your friends remember important events and good times spent together. From picture frames to a calendar or memory box, you can make projects that remind your friend of the most important part of your friendship: the experiences

you've shared, all the
things you have in common, and all the times you've been
there for each other.

Turn to the Best Times section of the book for cool party
ideas that get friends together for fun and creativity. Whether
there are two of you or 10, you'll find activities and projects
that you'll enjoy doing together. Swap spaces with your
friend for an afternoon and give her room a makeover featuring do-it-yourself projects. Have a craft night party where
each girl uses the same materials to make her own unique
accessories. Make two-of-a-kind accessories with a one-of-a-
kind friend, or host a spa party where you and your friends
turn your kitchen into a cosmetics lab, making all-natural
beauty products. Whatever activity and projects you pick,
you're guaranteed to have the best of times.

Whether you're making projects for friends or with them, take
your time and enjoy yourself! Improvise and add your own style
and flair to the ideas you see here. Use your imagination to create the very best treasures
for the best of friends.

best gifts

You've probably heard the expression, "Friendship is about give and take." Well, this section of the book is about the give part. You rely on your friends everyday: for advice, encouragement, and companionship. You don't have to wait for birthdays or holidays to show them how much they mean to you. When you get an urge to make something fun and new, why not make something from this section of the book and give it to a friend as a gift? Do you know someone who loves traveling and learning about different places and cultures? The projects in the *Worldly Girl* section are perfect for a girl with a sense of adventure. Does your friend love a good book? You don't have to write a novel for her—the projects in the *Book Lover* section show that you can enjoy a good book without even reading it! Does your friend have a passion for fashion? Make her something one-of-a-kind from the *Fashion Diva* section. Don't feel too badly if you love the project you made so much that you can't part with it. Just make two so you can each have one!

wordly girl

She's the first person you've met who *really* loves sushi. She can say "nice to meet you" in five different languages, and her list of places to go is a mile long. If you've got a friend who's always up for exploring and discovering the world, the projects in this section of the book are just right for her. They're exotic and intriguing, just like your friend, but lucky for you, they're also easy to make.

going places purse

Paris, London, New York, Rio—A girl can dream, right? Find a map of your friend's dream destination (sometimes maps come free in travel books or magazines). Make the map into a purse so she can fantasize about walking down Broadway as she's walking down the hall to class.

You Will Need

Subway map or other map

Iron-on vinyl*

Iron-on interfacing*

Iron

Pinking shears*

Silver grommets*

Grommet setter*

Hammer (for use with grommets)

Sewing machine

Ball chain**

Ball chain closure ball**

Pliers

*Available at fabric stores
**Available at hardware stores

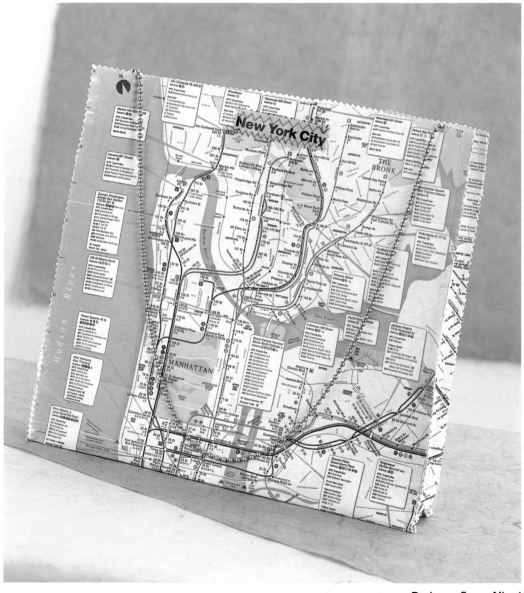

Designer: Sonya Nimri

1. Iron the interfacing to the back side of your map moving from the north side of the map to the south. The interfacing will be narrower than the map, so make sure you attach it to the portion of the map that you want showing on the purse.

2. Iron the vinyl to the printed side of the map, running north to south again, covering the same area you did in step 1.

3. Use your pinking shears to cut two pieces of the map for the front and back of the purse. For this purse, we cut 14 x 18-inch (35.6 x 45.7 cm) rectangles, but you can choose any shape or size.

4. Cut two identical pieces for the sides of the purse. For this purse, the two side pieces are 5 x 18 inches (12.7 x 45.7 cm).

5. Cut one piece for the bottom of the purse. For this purse, the bottom piece is 5 x 14 inches (12.7 x 35.6 cm).

6. Following the manufacturer's instructions, place two grommets about 1 inch (2.5 cm) from the top of each side piece, centered about 5 inches (12.7 cm) apart.

7. Sew the sides of the purse together, ¼ inch (6 mm) away from edges. The best method is to sew one side piece to the back and front first, then add the bottom piece, then the final side, top first, sewing down toward the bottom.

8. Run your ball chain through each grommet, then close the end off with the ball closure on the inside of the purse using the pliers.

Designer: Joan Morris

world tour frame

This frame is like a trip around the world without ever leaving your hometown. It makes a great present for a friend who loves to travel and is even more special if you use it for a picture of a trip you took together. If you don't have a stamp collection, check out flea markets and online auctions for a great selection of stamps from far-away places.

Wooden frame with wide border

Stamps from around the world

Decoupage glue

Small paintbrush

Clear polyurethane spray

1. Lay out your stamps on a table and pick your favorites. Look for ones with a lot of color and images that will jump out at you from a distance. Try separating the stamps by colors for a strong visual impact.

2. Decide where the bottom of the frame is and always keep that in mind when placing your stamps. Starting at one outside corner, paint a little decoupage glue onto the frame and the back of the stamp. The glue is somewhat slow-setting, so you have time to slide the stamp around until you get the look you want. As you continue to add stamps, consider your design. For this frame, we used stamps with pinks and purples toward the center of the frame and blues and greens around the edge. Position some stamps straight and some angled. If a stamp is stubborn and won't stay in place just apply more glue to its backside and rub it into place. The glue will dry clear. When you reach the edges of the frame, wrap the stamps around the edge.

Work your way around the frame until you've covered it completely. If you see any blank spots or don't like a certain stamp, just place another stamp over it.

3. When you are satisfied with the look of your frame, let it dry overnight. Spray it with a couple of coats of polyurethane to prevent the stamps from tearing or peeling off.

Autumn & Pearl

Friends for one year

Pearl's fun.

She's a lot like me and we like hanging out and being crazy together.

The most important things in a friendship: Friends should listen, have fun together, and be crazy together.

How Do You Say Friend

A worldly girl needs to know how to say "friend" in many different languages. Here's how you say it in languages from all over the world:

Arabic	Sadik
Croatian	prijatelj (m), prijateljica (f)
Farsi	Ra'figh
Finnish	Ystävä
French	Un ami (m), une amie (f)
Greek	O fi'los
Hawaiian	Hoaloha
Hebrew	Chaver (m), chavera (f)
Hindi	Dost, mitra
Hungarian	Barát
Icelandic	Vinur
Indonesian	Teman
Italian	Amico (m), Amica (f)
Japanese	Tomodachi
Korean	Chin-gu
Polish	Przyjaciel/ (m), przyjaciól/ka (f)
Russian	Drug
Spanish	El amigo (m), la amiga (f)
Swahili	Rafiki
Tagalog	Kaib'igan
Thai	Phuan
Turkish	Arkadas
Urdu	Aashna
Vietnamese	Ba'n
Zulu	Umngane

Designer: Therese de la Baton Rouge

A tasteful treat, this stationery kit comes in a take-out sushi tray. Use chopstick wrappers, Chinese restaurant placemats, or even origami papers to create unique stickers that transform plain note cards into super-special stationery. You'll need to buy a sticker machine for this project (or borrow one), but you'll certainly use it over and over again!

You Will Need

Plastic sushi tray

Note cards and envelopes

Chopstick wrappers

Asian decorative papers

Scissors

Sticker machine*

Metallic gel pens

Asian-inspired scrapbook embellishments (optional)

*Available at craft stores

1. Wash and dry the sushi tray! Fishy-smelling stationery is not the sort of gift you'd like to receive, now is it?

2. Take your tray to the craft store when you buy your note cards. You want to be sure that the envelopes and cards will comfortably fit inside the tray.

3. Carefully separate the two layers of your chopstick wrappers.

4. Place one side of the wrapper in the sticker machine to create a long sticker.

5. Trim the sticker to fit on your cards.

6. Run a strip of decorative paper through the sticker machine.

7. Stick the decorative paper to a card, then stick the wrapper on top of it. Decorate all of your cards this way.

8. To decorate the gel pens, wrap a piece of decorative paper around the pen to figure out the right size, then cut it to fit. Run the paper through the sticker machine, then wrap it around the pen.

9. Make stickers with your decorative paper, but don't stick them to anything. Put them in the tray with the stationery and pens. They'll make fun seals to put on the envelopes.

10. Decorate the clear lid of the tray with Asian-theme stickers.

cartouche necklace

Designer: Kathyrn Temple

A cartouche is an Egyptian nameplate written in ancient hieroglyphics. Back in the time of the pharaohs, only high-ranking people or royals wore them, but you can easily make one for your friend to make her feel like a queen. It's fun to learn about hieroglyphic symbols, too. Knowing all those secret symbols can come in handy when you're writing private notes!

You Will Need

- Printout or copy of cartouche symbols (see page 21)
- Scissors
- Craft glue
- Piece of cardstock
- Fine-tipped gold paint pen
- Metal foil tape*
- Acrylic varnish
- Small paintbrush
- Thumbtack
- Jump ring**
- Needle-nose pliers
- Necklace chain**

*Available at hardware stores or home centers
**Available at craft stores

1. Do an online search of the word cartouche. You'll find several sites where you can type in your friend's name (or your own) to get the hieroglyphic translation. Print out the name. If you don't have access to a computer with online service, make photocopies of the guide on page 21 and cut out the symbols you need. Whether you're using a printout or a photocopy from this book, you'll probably have to make another photocopy to reduce the size of the images to a good size for your necklace.

2. Once you've got the symbols arranged vertically in the size you want for the necklace, cut out the name and glue it to a small piece of cardstock or other heavy paper, leaving a 1-inch (2.5 cm) margin around the name. The cartouche should be strong enough that it doesn't bend or rip easily.

3. Use the paint pen to paint the background of the cartouche. Paint carefully around the hieroglyphics so you can still read them. Let the paint dry.

4. Cut the cartouche into an oval shape like you see in the picture.

5. Paint a layer of acrylic varnish over the cartouche. Allow it to dry.

6. Cut a rectangle of cardstock or thin cardboard a little wider than the oval you cut in step 4. You'll mount the oval to this piece later.

7. Cover the rectangle with metal-foil tape, tucking the ends around the back.

8. When the varnish on the cartouche has dried, glue it to the metal-foil covered rectangle.

9. Use a thumbtack to poke a hole at the top.

10. Use needle-nose pliers to open up a jump ring. Feed the jump ring through the hole and close it with the pliers. Run the chain through the jump ring.

Write Like an Egyptian

What may look like a row of simple pictures to you was a vast and complex language to ancient Egyptians. Long a mystery to modern scientists, hieroglyphics are Egyptian writing characters used for ceremonial and religious inscriptions, as well as for recording historic events.

Little was known about this form of writing until the *Rosetta Stone* was discovered in 1799. The stone was engraved with three forms of writing on its surface: hieroglyphics, demotic Egyptian (a cursive form of hieroglyphics used for everyday writing), and Greek. The stone allowed Egyptologists to translate the hieroglyphics by comparing them to Greek, a language they understood.

There are two basic types of hieroglyphic symbols: ideograms (pictures that represent a specific object, person, or place) and phonograms (signs or letters that represent sounds and are used for spelling just like our modern-day alphabet). There are hundreds of hieroglyphic pictures, but most Egyptologists agree that there are 25 basic Egyptian letters. Each of these letters can be written in a number of different ways, and some symbols can represent a combination of two or even three letters. While Egyptian hieroglyphics were often written right to left, they can be displayed in a variety of ways: from left to right, horizontally, or vertically. One quick clue to the orientation of the letters is that the signs usually face the beginning of the inscription.

A cartouche is a special way of inscribing someone's name with hieroglyphics. Letters are organized, both horizontally and vertically, within a drawn loop of rope with a knot at one end. The oval loop represents the universe, and the pharaoh's name (or in this case, your friend's name) inside represents his (or your friend's!) rule over the universe.

Here is a list of the basic Egyptian hieroglyphic alphabet you can use to create a cartouche:

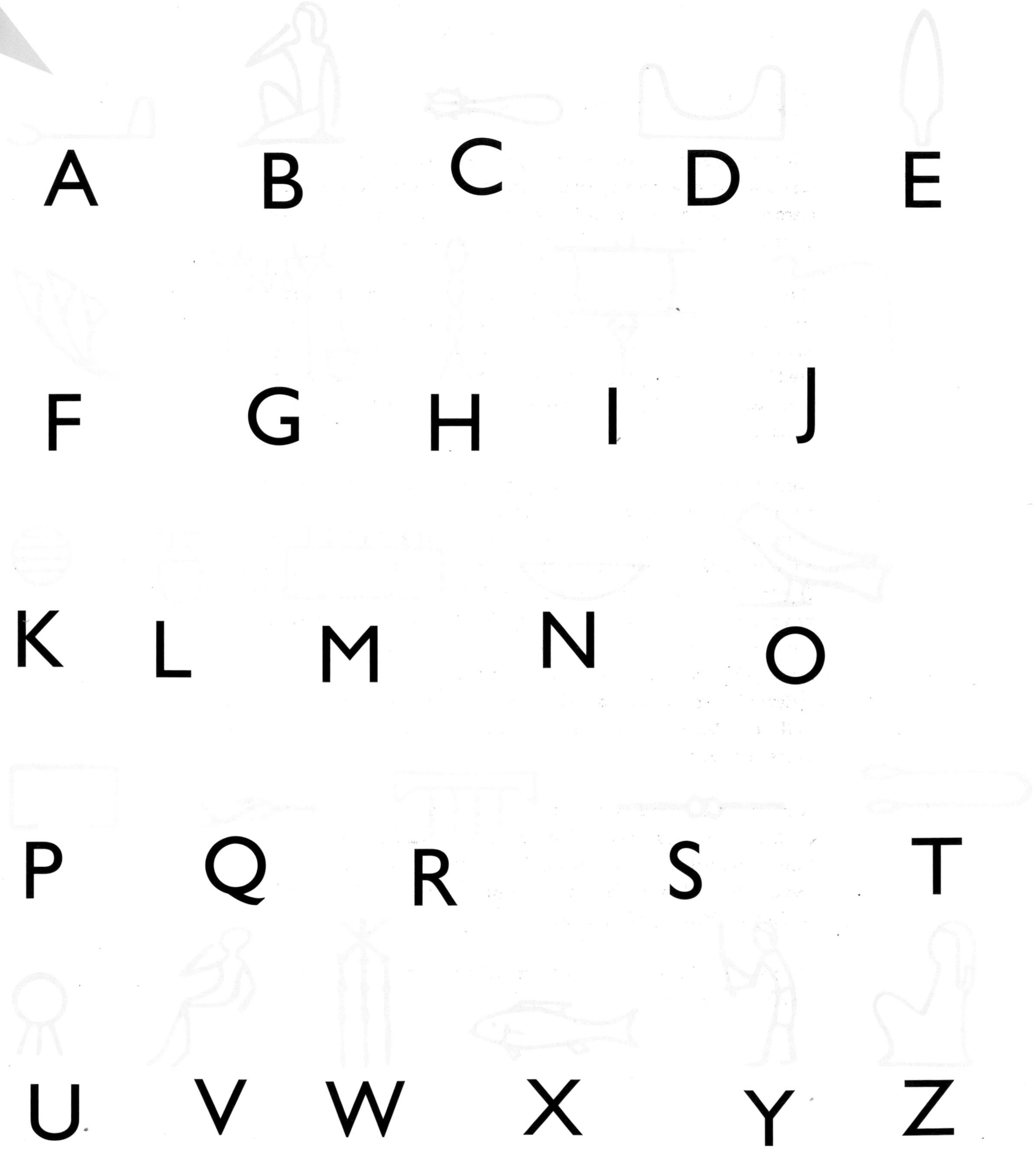

A B C D E

F G H I J

K L M N O

P Q R S T

U V W X Y Z

Designer: Joan Morris

chinese zodiac sign necklace

Is your friend a rat, a monkey, or a dog? Find out her Chinese zodiac sign and make her a necklace featuring her zodiac animal. It's fun to read about the personality traits assigned to each animal and it's easy to find images of each of the animals. You can even get them for free on placemats at Chinese restaurants.

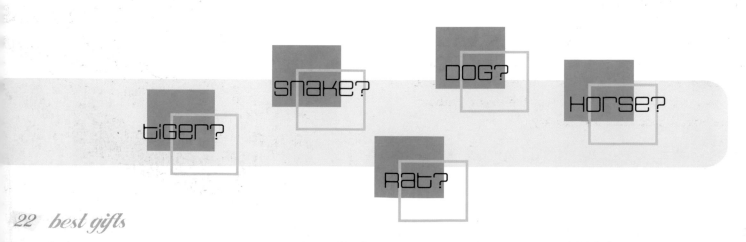

TiGER?   SNAKE?   DOG?   HORSE?   RAT?

You Will Need

Microscope slides*

Scrap paper

Pencil

Scissors

Images from magazines, color copies, or Chinese restaurant placemats or chopstick covers

Super-strong glue

1/2-inch (1.3 cm) copper or silver foil tape**

Frozen-treat stick

Needle-nose pliers

Eye pins (1 to 1 1/2 inches [2.4 to 3.8 cm] long)***

Jump rings***

Assorted beads***

Necklace cording or chain or ribbon

*Available at hobby stores
**Available at hardware stores
***Available at craft stores

1. Put a plain piece of paper under the microscope slide and draw around it, creating a template. Find images that you like and use the template to cut them to the correct size.

2. Turn each picture over and place a drop or two of glue on the back in the center. Place one eye pin on top of the picture so one eyelet extends above the picture and the other so it extends below. Place your second picture on top of the pins (front side facing up) and press in place. Let this dry. For a simple necklace without the eye pins, make a loop with a piece of ribbon and place the loose ends between the pictures so that the slide hangs from the loop. Or you can extend the ends of the ribbon out the bottom and tie knots in each end.

3. Create a sandwich by placing a slide on each side of the image. Cut two pieces of the foil tape the length of the long sides of the slides. Peel the backing off, and carefully apply the tape to one side of the glass then fold over to cover the other side. Rub out any wrinkles with the frozen-treat stick. The foil is sharp and can cut you, so don't rub it with your hands.

4. Cut two pieces of foil to cover the top and bottom of the slides. Fold the pieces in half and cut a small slit in the center of each. Peel the backing off the tape and place the slit over the eye pins and fold over the edges. Smooth with the frozen-treat stick if necessary.

5. Open a jump ring with the needle-nose pliers and place it in the top eye ring so you can run a cord or chain through it to hang the slide. If you're using a cord or ribbon, tie it over your head first to get the length right. If you're using a chain, attach neck closures to the ends.

6. You can add more jump rings with beads on them to the eye pin at the bottom of the necklace, or string beads onto an eye pin and attach them with pliers.

Variations

Don't limit yourself to the Chinese zodiac for this kind of necklace. You can use any kind of images. Look in books, magazines, online, or in your own photo album for cool images you'd like to feature in a necklace. Vertical ones are obviously better than horizontal ones. Try to think of front and backs that will match, but are not the same. For example, you could use a picture of a dog's face on the front of the necklace and his tail on the back.

The Chinese Zodiac

According to the Chinese system of astrology, knowing the year of a person's birth can tell you a lot more than just her age. Each year has an animal sign assigned to it, and some people believe that those born under a certain animal sign will have that animal's characteristics. Some people even think that the qualities of the sign governing a given year will affect events that happen during those 365 days.

Although the horoscopes based on the Chinese zodiac aren't taken seriously, the signs serve a useful social function for indirectly finding out people's ages. Instead of asking someone bluntly how old they are (which might be considered rude) you could ask for their animal sign and use a little common sense and math wizardry to deduce their age.

The origins of the Chinese zodiac remain uncertain, but one legend claims that Buddha called all the animals of China to his bedside, and only 12 came. To honor their devotion, Buddha created a year for each animal.

Monkey 1980, 1992, 2004

Witty, popular, good-humored, versatile, clever
Most compatible with Dragons and Rats. Least compatible with Tigers.

Some well-known Monkeys: *Julius Caesar, Betsy Ross, Elizabeth Taylor, Leonardo da Vinci, Eleanor Roosevelt*

Rooster 1981, 1993, 2005

Aggressive, alert, perfectionist, fearless, critical
Most compatible with Snakes and Oxen. Least compatible with Rabbits.

Roosters to crow about: *Amelia Earhart, Rudyard Kipling, Groucho Marx, Catherine the Great*

Dog 1982, 1994, 2006

Loyal, conservative, honest, sympathetic, practical
Most compatible with Horses and Tigers. Least compatible with Dragons.

A few lucky Dogs: *Socrates, Benjamin Franklin, Winston Churchill, Jane Goodall*

Pig/Boar 1983, 1995, 2007

Caring, industrious, home-loving, honest
Most compatible with Rabbits and Sheep. Least compatible with Boars.

Born in the year of the Pig: *Ernest Hemingway, Lucille Ball, Albert Schweitzer*

Mouse/Rat 1984, 1996, 2008

Charming, creative, bright, thrifty
Most compatible with Dragons and Monkeys. Least compatible with Horses.

Some famous Rats: *William Shakespeare, Mata Hari, Wolfgang Amadeus Mozart, George Washington*

Ox 1985, 1997, 2009

Dependable, methodical, reliable, stubborn, persistent.
Most compatible with Snakes and Roosters. Least compatible with Sheep.

Oxen through the ages: *Napoleon, Rosa Parks, Vincent van Gogh, Walt Disney*

Tiger 1986, 1998, 2010

Sincere, dynamic, warm, leader, fiery-tempered
Most compatible with Horses and Dogs. Least compatible with Monkeys.

Well-known Tigers include: *Beatrix Potter, Marilyn Monroe, Judy Blume, Marco Polo, Dwight D. Eisenhower*

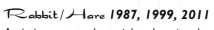

Rabbit/Hare 1987, 1999, 2011

Artistic, smart, clear-sighted, quiet, humble
Most compatible with Sheep and Boars. Least compatible with Roosters.

Some Rabbits: *Madame Curie, Albert Einstein, Queen Victoria, Andy Warhol, Marie Antoinette, Agatha Christie*

Dragon 1988, 2000, 2012

Lucky, flamboyant, imaginative
Most compatible with Monkeys and Rats. Least compatible with Dogs.

A few Dragons: *Sigmund Freud, Dr. Seuss, John Lennon, Joan of Arc, Mae West*

Snake 1989, 2001, 2013

Intelligent, refined, discreet, sophisticated, tactful, shrewd
Most compatible with Roosters and Oxen. Least compatible with Sheep.

Born under the sign of the Snake: *Abraham Lincoln, Queen Elizabeth I, Anne Frank, Charles Darwin, Mahatma Gandhi, Edgar Allan Poe, Martin Luther King, Jr.*

Horse 1990, 2002, 2014

Sociable, competitive, stubborn, impulsive, sensitive
Most compatible with Tigers and Dogs. Least compatible with Rats.

Some fresh Horses: *Louisa May Alcott, Sandra Day O'Connor, Rembrandt van Rijn, Theodore Roosevelt*

Sheep/Goat 1991, 2003, 2015

Artistic, fastidious, indecisive, steadfast, patient
Most compatible with Boars and Rabbits. Least compatible with Oxen.

Sheep that stand out from the crowd: *Mark Twain, Orville Wright, Michelangelo*

book lover

She's the one you turn to when you need a book review because she's read *everything*. She'll stay up half the night to finish a good book because she just can't put it down. If this describes your friend, make her one of the projects in this section. Some are made for books, some are made out of books, but all will be appreciated by a true *bibliophile* (you guessed it—that's another word for book lover).

Designer: Joan Morris

a novel idea purse

This may be the only case when it's actually OK to judge a book by its cover. It's fun shopping in second-hand bookstores for the perfect book to make into a purse. Choose one with great colors, interesting designs, or a title that will be funny or meaningful to your friend. Find fabric that coordinates, and you'll make a page-turner into a head-turner!

Hardcover book

Measuring tape or ruler

Craft knife

Scissors

½-yard (45.8 cm) canvas or heavy fabric

Matching thread

Sewing machine

Pencil

Iron and ironing board

Straight pins

Super-strong craft glue

Frozen-treat stick

1. You may need an adult to help you with this first step. Take the pages out of the book by cutting along the inside edge of the spine with a craft knife, carefully avoiding the covers. The pages will come out in one piece.

2. Cut two pieces of the fabric about 3 ½ x 15 inches (8.9 x 38 cm) long. These are the straps.

3. Place your fabric inside the book cover. You'll want it to cover the inside of the book, plus a 3 ½-inch (8.9 cm) hem on the top of each side. The cloth sides of the purse which extend between the two covers should each be about 3 ½ inches (8.9 cm) wide on each side for a total of 7 inches (17.8 cm) of fabric between the two covers (Figure 1).

4. Fold both strap pieces right sides together lengthwise. Machine stitch the length of the strap with a ½-inch (1.3 cm) seam allowance. At one end of each piece, stitch the short-end opening closed.

5. Use the pencil to push the stitched short end through the whole piece to turn the straps right side out. Press the straps so that the seams are centered on the tube of fabric.

Figure 1

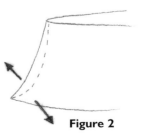

Figure 2

6. Fold the large cut piece of fabric in half, right sides together. Machine stitch the short sides together with a ¹/₂-inch (1.3 cm) seam allowance, leaving the wide top side open as the opening of the purse.

7. Press the seams open. To create the bottom of the bag, make a triangle at the bottom of the seam with the seam in the center, and stitch across the triangle at the 1-inch (2.5 cm) point (Figure 2). Repeat for the other side of the bag. Cut off the extra fabric at the end of the triangle.

8. Place the sewn pouch inside the book and fold down to the inside until it's even with the top of the book. Press these seams and pin if you need to. Take the pouch out of the book. Fold the raw edges under a ¹/₂-inch (1.3 cm) hem. Press and pin in place.

9. Machine stitch all the way around the hem you made in step 8.

10. Decide where you want to place the handles. Pin them in place on the outside of the bag. Make the handle 10 inches (25.4 cm) long from top edge to top edge. Keeping the seams on the inside, machine stitch a 2-inch (5.2 cm) long rectangle to hold the handle in place. At the point where the handle meets the top of the bag, you can run the sewing machine back and forth to give the handle more strength.

11. To glue the pouch to the book cover, use the frozen-treat stick to spread the glue evenly on one inside cover of the book first. Carefully lay the pouch in place. Press the pouch in place starting at the top of the pouch moving down to the bottom. Let it dry for a while.

12. Apply glue to the spine of the book and the second cover the same way you did in step 11. Start at the top of the second cover and work your way down to the spine. If there are any lumps, just keep pressing the fabric into the book until it flattens out.

Designer: Kathryn Temple

secret stash box

With all the books on your friend's bookshelf, no one will suspect that there's more to this one than meets the eye. A secret stash disguised as a book, it's perfect for hiding a private journal or anything else your friend wants to keep away from prying eyes.

Hardcover book

Craft knife (optional)

Ruler or measuring tape

Shallow cardboard box, slightly smaller than the dimensions of the book and approximately the same thickness

Long strip of paper

Scissors

Ribbon for trim

1. Remove the pages from the book with your hands or a craft knife (you may need an adult to help).

2. Measure and cut a piece of paper the same thickness of the edge of the box and long enough to wrap around all four sides.

3. Glue the strip of paper around the edge of the box. Make sure the ends of the strip fall on one of the long edges of the box. Then make sure that this side of the box faces the spine of the book.

4. Glue the box to the back cover of the book. Press it down firmly. You may want to put something heavy inside the box to weigh it down while it's drying.

5. Decorate the inside of the box with ribbon for trim or whatever else you like.

glam slam book

Designer: Emma Pearson

This slam book is cleverly disguised as a purse to keep it super secret. You or your friend can just slip the strap over your shoulder as you walk between classes, looking stylish and keeping your notes well hidden.

You Will Need

Nonspiral-bound notebook

Piece of cardboard or old box

Marker

Craft knife

Ruler

Fabric of your choice

Scissors

Spray adhesive

Hot glue gun and glue sticks

Pompoms or other trim

Craft felt squares

1 yard (91.4 cm) thin cotton cord

Beads of your choice

Masking tape

Super-strong glue

Piece of ribbon, about 3 inches (7.6 cm) long

Small piece of hook-and-loop tape

1. Center the notebook on a piece of cardboard, then fold the cardboard over the notebook, making sure that it reaches all the way around both sides. You'll need to make folds in the cardboard for the section that will cover the spine of the notebook.

2. On the cardboard, mark a shape with angled sides according to Figure 1.

3. Use a craft knife to cut out the piece of cardboard along the lines you drew in step 2 (you may need an adult to help). You should end up with a piece like Figure 2.

4. Before you glue the cardboard cover to the notebook you need to cover the cardboard with colored fabric. Lay the cardboard down centered on the fabric of your choice. Trace around the cardboard, adding a 1-inch (2.5 cm) "hem" on all sides. Cut out the fabric shape.

5. Spray the cardboard shape with spray adhesive, then carefully center it on the fabric, smoothing out any wrinkles as you press it in place. Wrap the "hem" around the sides of the cardboard. You'll need to cut little slits in the fabric on the corners and at the spine so that it doesn't bunch up (Figure 3).

6. Hot glue the pompom fringe to the inside cover of the cardboard, near the edge.

7. Cut out stars or shapes from felt and hot glue them to the fabric on the outside covers. Cut pompoms from your leftover fringe and glue them to the centers of the stars or shapes.

8. Measure a piece of cotton cord to run the length of the notebook's spine, around your shoulder, and back into the notebook as a strap. Cut the cord and double-knot it at one end.

9. Thread beads along the cord, leaving the cord that will go into the spine of the book unbeaded. In other words, subtract the measurement of the spine's length from the total measurement of the cord and string the beads up to that measurement.

10. Hot glue the strap to the inside of the cardboard cover so that the beaded portion of the strap shows on the outside. Use masking tape over the cord for an extra secure bond if you like (Figure 4).

11. Glue the notebook into the cardboard cover with super-strong glue.

12. Glue a small piece of hook-and-loop tape at the edge of what will be the back cover of the slam book.

13. Measure and cut a small piece of ribbon to extend from the front of the book to the back when the book is closed (on the open edge, not the spine edge).

14. Cut out two small felt shapes. Glue one to each end of the ribbon piece you cut in step 13.

15. Glue one of the felt shapes to the front of the book. On the back of the other felt shape, glue a piece of hook-and-loop tape that will attach to the one you glued on the back cover of the book. To close the book, just position the hook-and-loop pieces on top of each other.

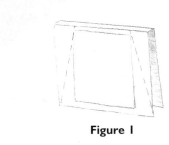

Figure 1

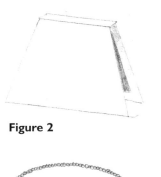

Figure 2

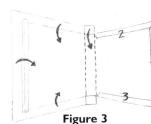

Figure 3

Figure 4

Slam Book Do's & Don'ts

- *Do* use an alias if you want to keep your identify hidden.

- *Don't* use a slam book to gossip or say mean things about others.

- *Do* ask meaningful questions that will encourage thought and discussion.

- *Do* develop a system for answering questions. For example, you can start every page with one question written on top and have all the answers to the question on a single page. Make it a rule that everyone must answer every question in the same order to avoid confusion.

- *Do* insist that everyone write a real answer, not just "I don't know."

Focus on Friends

Natasha & Niroshka

Friends since: Always—we're sisters!

She's well organized and funny.

We take care of each other.

The best thing about having a sister: It's better than having a brother!

Designer: Kathryn Temple

what's your sign? booklace

A "booklace" is a little book made into a necklace—the perfect gift for a friend who loves books. Fill each page of the book you make with information about your friend's zodiac sign. It's a great conversation starter!

Aries   Taurus   Gemini   Cancer   Leo   Virgo   Libra

Scorpio   Sagittarius   Capricorn   Aquarius   Pisces

You Will Need

- Pencil
- Scissors
- Cardstock
- Stapler
- Astrology book
- Colored vellum paper
- Metallic paint pen
- Cord or thin ribbon
- Beads
- Small hole punch or nail

1. Using Figure 1 as a guide, cut a piece of cardstock and fold it along the lines indicated. This will be the cover of your book.

2. Staple the bottom flap of the book cover in place. Don't worry about the staple showing—you'll cover it later.

3. Using Figure 2 as a guide, cut and fold the vellum for the accordion-fold pages inside the book. For this book-lace, we used vellum pages in two different colors.

4. Research the colors, personality traits, and gemstones associated with your friend's astrological sign. Use your metallic paint pen to write the information on different accordion pages. Tuck one of the vellum pieces inside the other if you're using two pieces.

5. Cut a small piece of cardstock into an oval, then decorate it with the symbol of your friend's astrological sign. Glue it over the staple you placed in step 2 to serve as a flap.

6. Use a small hole punch to punch a hole in the spine (the narrow top fold) of the card stock.

7. Feed the cord or narrow ribbon through the hole and tie a knot so that it doesn't slide through.

8. Add beads to decorate the cord.

9. Fit the pages inside the cardstock cover and tuck the cover under the zodiac-sign flap.

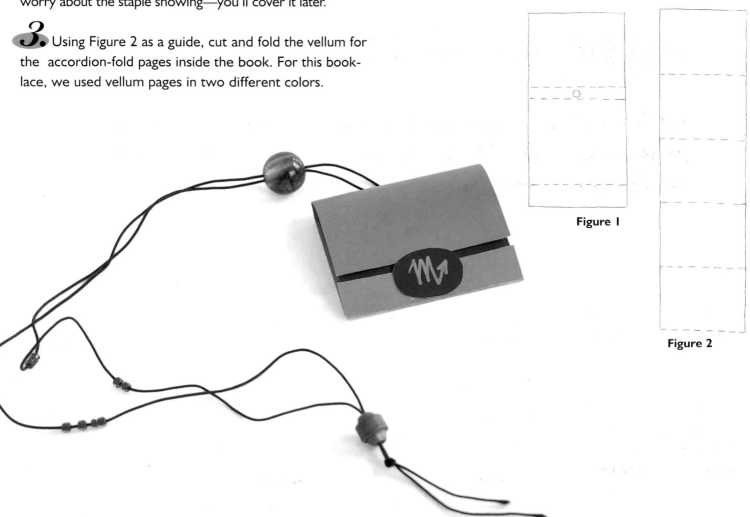

Figure 1

Figure 2

cute-as-a-button bookmark

A bookmark is a must-have accessory for every avid reader. That makes it a great idea for a handmade gift. This one is easy to make and hard to lose in the pages of a book.

You Will Need

Wire hanger

Wire cutters

Needle-nose pliers

Thin beading cord

Scissors

Buttons

Designer: Kathryn Temple

1. Get an adult to help you cut the long bottom of the wire hanger in half. Make a second cut about 2 inches (5.2 cm) from the bend in the hanger.

2. Use the needle-nose pliers to form a loop on each end of the hanger piece.

3. Cut a 14-inch (35.6 cm) piece of beading cord.

4. Thread the cord through one hole in a button, center it on the cord, and thread the other end through the second hole. (Note: if you are using buttons with four holes, make sure that you are threading through the holes across from, not next to, one another.)

5. Continue stacking buttons by threading the two lengths of cord through the holes in the buttons.

6. When you have reached the desired height, tie a double knot at the top of your stack.

7. Tie the stack to the loop on the hook end of the hanger piece.

Fashion Diva

She doesn't follow all the latest trends—she has her own personal style. She prefers clothes that are one-of-a-kind and out of the ordinary. You can always count on her to help you pull together a great outfit when you thought you had nothing to wear. If your friend has a flair for fashion, she'll love one of the projects in this section. Follow the instructions or use the ideas as a springboard to make your own amazing creations.

Designer: Joan Morris

dangly spangly sequin sandals

The sequins used for these sandals are called paillettes, which is the French word for sequins. You can find these sparkly little numbers at any craft store, just waiting to transform an ordinary pair of sandals into a must-have accessory for a fashion-savvy girl.

You Will Need

Sandals with thong upper

Paillettes (sequins) in two different colors*

Straight pins

Purple embroidery floss**

Scissors

Embroidery needle**

Thimble**

*Available at craft stores
**Available at fabric stores

1. Lay out your design on the sandals by pinning the paillettes onto the thong part. Start at the narrow part closest to the toe and move up to the widest part that goes on top of the foot. Alternate the colors of the paillettes for a more interesting design.

2. When you're happy with your design, leave it on one shoe to use as a guide. Thread the embroidery needle with about 3 feet (91.4 cm) of embroidery floss. Keep the thread doubled and knot the end. Starting at the narrow end of the thong, push the needle from the underside of the shoe through the hole in the paillette (use the thimble if it's difficult to get the needle through). Wrap the thread around the top of the paillette, back through the shoe, then back up under the paillette, then make a knot. This allows you to hide the knots under the paillettes, which is more comfortable than leaving them on the underside of the shoe.

3. To make the second row, place the next paillette in position and push the needle up through the hole and then back down. Repeat this row after row. At some point you will need to re-thread the needle. To do this, knot the piece you're using on the top side hidden under a paillette, and start with a new piece of embroidery floss. Repeat this at the end of your last row.

no-sew pursemat

Designer: Joan Morris

This chic bag is made from inexpensive plastic placemats with great designs on them and a few other easy-to-find materials. It's big enough to carry books and notebooks to school, but it would also make a great beach tote for a surfer girl or a beach bum.

You Will Need

3 vinyl placemats

Ruler

Scissors

11 grommets, each $\frac{3}{8}$ inch (9.5 mm) in diameter*

Grommet setter*

Pen

Craft knife

Hammer

Clear-drying craft glue

Wire cutter

Pliers

3 feet (91.4 cm) of $\frac{1}{16}$-inch (1.6 mm) cable**

4 sets of ferrule and stop (a kind of hardware), each $\frac{1}{16}$-inch (1.6 mm) in diameter **

28 round plastic beads, each $\frac{1}{2}$ inch (1.3 cm) in diameter

8 oblong plastic beads, each $\frac{3}{4}$ inch (1.9 cm) in diameter

*Available at fabric stores
**Available at hardware or home improvement stores

1. Position two placemats wrong sides together with the design right-side up on both placemats. Decide where you want to place the pocket for the purse and position the last placemat there.

2. Decide how tall you want the pocket to be. Use the ruler and a pen to mark where you'll cut the placemat for the pocket, then cut it along the line.

3. Near the top of each of the uncut placements which will be the sides of the purse, mark where you want to attach handles. Try to center them in from the edges, about 5 inches (12.7 cm) apart.

4. There are two parts to a grommet, a flat circle and one with a ridge. Lay one flat circle in position on the vinyl and draw the inside circle onto the vinyl. Use the craft knife to carefully cut around the inside (you may need an adult to help). From the right side of placemat, place the grommet with a ridge into the hole. Position the grommet on the anvil part of the grommet tool. Turn the placemat over and place the flat part of the grommet over the other placemat. Place the large end of the tool over the flat piece. Working on a firm surface, strike the grommet firmly with the hammer until the stem of the ridged piece rolls over the flat piece. This takes a few tries, but it will work eventually. Repeat this process until you've set two grommets for the handles in each side of the purse.

5. Place the two sides of the purse right sides together. Following step 4, place a grommet in each upper corner. This time you'll have to cut through two placemats instead of just one.

6. Place the pocket in position. Starting at the top corners of the pocket, mark and insert the grommets. This time, you're cutting through three placemats. Once the pocket is in place, set the grommets across the bottom.

7. Carefully run a thin bead of glue across the bottom and the sides of the pocket. Try to hide the glue in the design.

8. To make the handles, cut the cable in half with the wire cutters. String the beads onto each piece in a pattern you like, leaving room at each end for a loop.

9. Place the ferrule and stop on each end, small part first. Run the end through the grommet for handle. Bring the end back up and run it through the ferrule. Use the pliers to pinch together the ferrule which will hold the cable in position. Cut the excess cable with wire cutters. Repeat this for both handles.

henna stencil clothes

The unusual designs used to make temporary henna tattoos look just as great on clothes as they do on hands. You can buy rubber stencils of the designs online or at Indian markets, then spray paint through the stencils to create T-shirts or pants with exotic appeal.

You Will Need

Solid-colored T-shirt and/or pants

Scraps of cardboard to place over the clothes

Scissors

Spray adhesive

Assorted henna stencils (any stencil will do, but henna stencils come pre-sticky)*

Spray paint

Paper

Pencil

Masking tape

*Available from online henna suppliers or Indian markets

Designer: Joan Morris

1. Wash and dry the clothing you want to use.

2. Cut a piece of cardboard the size of the front of the T-shirt. Spray the cardboard with spray adhesive. Just a light coat will work.

3. Center the T-shirt over the cardboard making sure that the spray adhesive sticks to it and holds it in place.

4. Place your stencil on a piece of paper. Draw around it. Cut out the outline around the stencil. This will be used to keep the spray paint off the rest of your shirt.

5. Place the stencil in position on the front of the T-shirt. Place the cut-out piece of paper over the stencil so only the stencil is showing. Tape additional pieces of paper over the shirt as needed to protect it from the spray paint. You may want to practice spraying through the stencil on a scrap of fabric first to see how much paint comes out and to avoid paint drips.

6. With even strokes, lightly spray the stencil until you see that the shirt underneath is covered with color.

7. Very carefully remove the paper from the stencil, then remove the stencil. This can be messy, so be sure you have a place to put the painted stencil. Clean it with soap and water. Not all the paint will come off, but it is still reusable after it dries.

8. Once the first sprayed area dries, you can start on the next stencil, if you're using one, following the same directions.

9. When the spray paint has dried, pull the T-shirt off the cardboard. Wait a few days before washing it. Turn the shirt inside out to wash.

Variation

With some kinds of fabric, a little excess spray paint around the stenciled image looks good. Experiment to see what looks best on the material you're using.

Night of Henna

The intriguing patterns you see on pages 44-45 are traditional designs used to apply henna to women's hands, arms, and feet as temporary tattoos. Henna has been used for thousands of years in ritual celebrations in Mediterranean cultures, the Middle East, and India. In many countries, women hold a "Night of Henna" celebration for a bride just before her wedding. The henna designs, which vary from region to region, are meant to express happiness, protect the wearer, or bring good luck. In North Africa, the designs are often geometric, whereas in India and Pakistan they tend to be more fanciful, featuring paisleys, birds, or lacy patterns. In Arab countries, the designs often feature flowers, vines, or scrolls.

Henna kits are available through online sources or can be found at health food or craft stores. Why not throw a Night of Henna party for your friends to celebrate a birthday or other special event? It's fun to paint the designs on each other's feet, hands, or arms, and as you can see from the project on pages 44-45, henna stencils can also be used to paint designs onto your clothes with acrylic or spray paint. Copy the designs here on page 140 or make your own. Use the recipe below to mix your henna.

Henna Recipe

1 teaspoon (5 g) powdered henna
2 teaspoons (10 ml) bottled water or brewed dark tea cooled to room temperature
5 drops eucalyptus oil
1 teaspoon (5 ml) lemon juice

Mix the henna powder, water, eucalyptus oil, and lemon juice in a glass bowl, stirring to remove the lumps. Let the paste sit for a few hours before using. Apply the henna with a toothpick, pastry bag and tip, or small plastic bag with one tip snipped off.

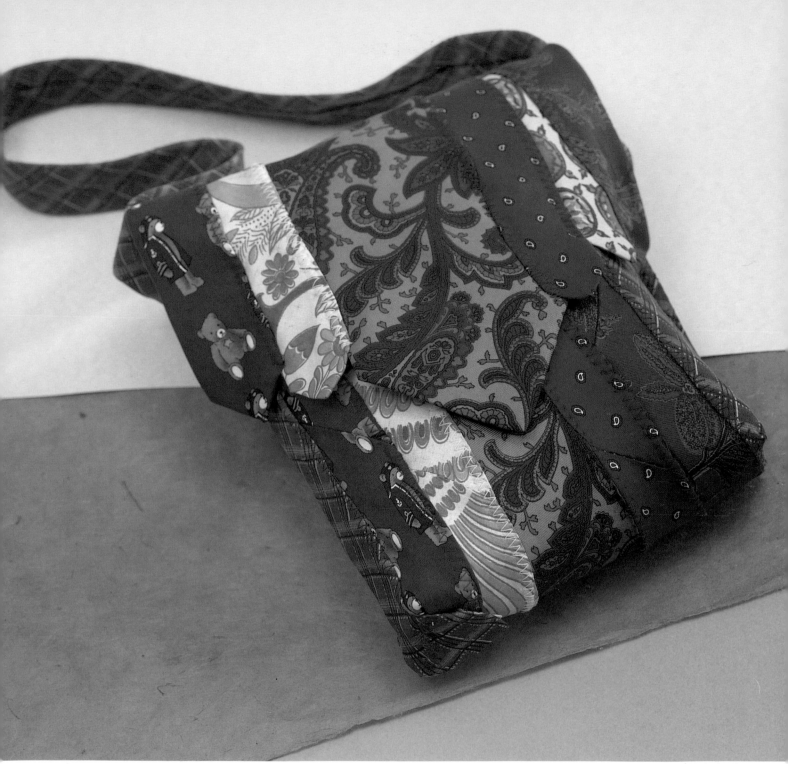

Designer: Sonya Nimri

my tie purse

Why should guys always get to wear the ties? This cool purse turns old neckties (available at thrift stores or in your dad's closet) into a fabulous fashion accessory and a great surprise gift for a friend.

8 neckties

Matching thread

Sewing machine

Measuring tape

Scissors

Needle and thread

1. Pick your favorite tie out of the bunch. This one will be at the center of your purse. Arrange 6 of the remaining ties around the center tie, three on each side.

2. When you've got the design that you like, start to sew them together one at a time. Starting with the center tie, sew the narrow end to one of the adjacent ties using a zigzag stitch. Stop when you come to the point on the wide end of the tie. Your stitches should overlap both ties, but try to keep your ties straight or they will veer off to the right or left. Continue sewing each tie to the side of the next until you have a long strip of ties. Instead of being a perfect rectangle, it will taper into a V-shape where the point of the center tie tapers.

3. Measure from the point of the center tie up 24 inches (61 cm) and cut off the bottom of the strip so that it's straight across and not so tapered. Turn the raw edge over and sew a 1-inch (2.5 cm) hem.

4. With your strip facing right side out, fold the straight edge up about 8 inches (20.3 cm) to form the pouch. Now you have a 16-inch (40.6 cm) long flap and an 8-inch (20.3 cm) long pouch. Sew the pouch side onto the flap side on one side. That leaves one side of the pouch open.

5. You still have one tie left. Use it to close up the open side and form a strap. Position the narrowest side of the strap tie on the open side of the pouch. The point will overlap the bottom edge of the pouch a bit. Start sewing the tie to one side of the pouch at the position where the tie comes out of the point all the way up to the place where the flap folds over (Figure 1). Repeat on the other side of the strap tie to close the pouch.

6. Hand sew the free end of the strap to the other side of the purse about 1 inch (2.5 cm) from the top (Figure 2).

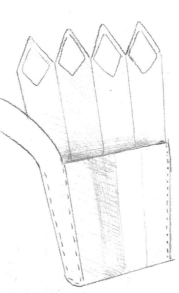

Figure 1

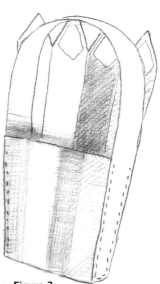

Figure 2

fasten your neat belt

Designer: Joan Morris

Another fun use for a tie—and you don't even need a sewing machine for this one. Find an old necktie with a great pattern and take it from formal to funky with a few simple cuts and stitches.

You Will Need

Measuring tape

Necktie

2 D rings*

Sewing needle and matching thread

Scissors

Straight pins

*Available at craft stores

1. Get your friend's waist measurement and add 14 inches (35.6 cm) to that measurement. Write down the total. From the skinny tip of the tie, measure up to the total measurement you took and cut the tie at that point. You'll use the wide end of the tie later, so put it aside for now.

2. Fold 2 inches (5.2 cm) of the cut end of the tie over the two D rings. Fold the end under about $^1/_2$ inch (1.3 cm) and pin in place.

3. Hand stitch the fold down, starting at one side near the D rings, across the bottom of the fold, and back up the other side to the D rings. This will keep the D rings in place.

4. From the tip at the wide end of the tie, measure up 12 inches (30.5 cm) and cut.

5. You now have two tie pieces. One has the D rings on one end and one free side. The other has the wide tie point on one end and one free side. Line up the two free sides so that the wrong side of the tie piece with the D rings meets the right side of the tie piece with the wide tie point. Fold under the raw edge of the piece with the wide point and wrap the fabric around the open end of the other piece, pinning it in place.

6. Hand stitch the two tie pieces together, hiding the stitches if you can. Stitch down about 2 inches (5.2 cm).

7. At the point where the skinny and wide points of the ties meet, hand stitch to keep the skinny tie from flapping out when the belt is worn.

flashy fleecey boa scarf

For a friend with a flair for the dramatic, this scarf is the ultimate accessory. If you've never sewn before, this is the perfect project for learning—you only have to sew a single straight line.

You Will Need

Scissors

Measuring tape

Sewing machine and thread

Fleece in two colors

1. Measure and cut two pieces of fleece, each about 10 x 50 inches (25.4 cm x 1.2 m).

2. Lay the two pieces on top of each other and machine stitch down the center, catching both pieces in your stitches.

3. Starting at one edge of the joined piece, cut through both pieces of fleece at $1/4$-inch (6 mm) intervals to create the fringe. Cut from the loose end, stopping about $1/2$ inch (1.3 cm) out from the stitch line. When you're finished cutting on one side, repeat the process on the other side (Figure 1).

Designer: Emma Pearson

Figure 1

Designer: Emma Pearson

cute boots

Hiking boots and fashion aren't usually mentioned in the same sentence. But these boots bring the two very different ideas together with fantastic results. With little more than a can of spray paint and some beads you can make these for a friend so she can hit the trail in style.

You Will Need

Pair of boots

Shoelaces

Acrylic paint

Paintbrushes (small)

Colored spray paint

Wire beads, charms, and bells

Pliers

1. Make sure the boots are clean and dry before spray painting. Remove the laces and pack the inside of the boots with old newspaper so that you don't get paint inside them.

2. Spray paint boots evenly in a well ventilated space on top of old newspapers or garbage bags. Leave to dry. This may take longer than the can suggests.

3. Once the boots are completely dry, paint on designs with acrylic paint. Randomly make dots over the boot with one color for the centers of the flowers. Paint even strokes around the dot with another color to make petals.

4. Once these flower designs dry, make the bead ornaments. Use the pliers to cut the wire into two 3-to 4-inch (7.6 cm to 10.2 cm) lengths. Make a small loop on one end of each wire to prevent the beads from coming off.

5. Thread the wires with colored beads and/or charms. Leave enough wire to form a loop on the other end of each wire. Twist the end around a few times to secure the loop.

6. Thread the bead ornaments through the laces.

lamin-art collage necklace

A few magazines, some jewelry findings, and a laminating machine—imagine the possibilities! Make a beautiful collage, then take it to a copier shop—most have laminating machines that you can walk right up and use. Cut your laminated collage into shapes of all kinds, then punch holes in the shapes to make a necklace, bracelet, belt, or even earrings. You'll have an awsome accessory in minutes.

You Will Need

Old magazines

Scissors

Office paper

Glitter

Glue stick

Pouch laminator*

Needle-nose pliers

Hole punch

Jump rings**

12mm lobster clasp**

*Available for use at copier shops
**Available at craft stores

Designer: Emma Pearson

1. Make a collage on both sides of your paper. Use magazine pictures or whatever images you like and glue them to the paper with a glue stick. Sprinkle a layer of glitter on top of the collage if you like.

2. When you're happy with the way your collage looks, take it to a copier shop and run it through the pouch laminator, following the instructions provided.

3. Cut out shapes from your laminated sheet. Circles, hearts, squares, or stars look great for jewelry. Try to keep the shapes to no more than 1 inch (2.5 cm) in diameter.

4. Use a hole punch to make holes near the edges of each shape to accommodate the jump rings that will hold the necklace together.

5. Start stringing the laminated shapes together with jump rings, one on each side of each shape. For a necklace, make a chain, approximately 15 inches (38 cm) long.

6. At one end of the chain, attach one lobster clasp and on the opposite end attach a jump ring.

no sweat purse

No money for expensive silky fabric? No sweat. Use an old pair of nylon running pants from your closet or a thrift store to make this adorable purse. The fabric looks like silk, and since the pants already have seams, it's easy to sew the rest together. Beads and fringe in coordinating colors will complete the transformation from sporty to stylish.

Designer: Kathryn Temple

Nylon running pants with gathered ankle

Needle and matching thread or sewing machine

Scissors

Fringe*

Seam ripper**

Needle-nose pliers

Necklace-size memory wire***

Beads

*Available at craft stores
**Available at fabric stores
***Available at bead stores

1. Cut the bottom from a pair of running pants about 12 inches (30.5 cm) from the ankle. Remove the lining if necessary.

2. Flip the fabric inside out and pin fringe inside the cut edge. The ribbon-like edge of the fringe should point toward the cut edge of the pants; the fringe edge should point toward the gathered ankle opening. Sew the fringe in place.

3. Sew the seam closed. Make sure your stitches are very close together, so that small things won't fall out of the purse when you use it.

4. Flip the bag right-side out.

5. Use the seam ripper to cut a slit on the inside edge of the ankle opening. Repeat on the other side of the opening. Remove the elastic if there is any.

6. Cut two equal lengths of memory wire. Each should be long enough to make one complete circle for a handle plus about 2 inches (5.2 cm) extra.

7. Use the needle-nose pliers to form a loop on one end of each of the wire pieces.

8. Thread each wire with beads.

9. Use the needle nose pliers to form a loop on the other end of the wire. Trim off any excess wire.

10. Feed the beaded wire through one slit in the ankle hem, then the other.

11. Use the pliers to interlock the end-loops on the wire, then scoot the beaded loop back a few inches so the end-loops are concealed by fabric.

12. Repeat with second beaded loop on the other side of the purse.

Clothes Swap Night!

Have you ever heard the expression "one man's trash is another man's treasure"? It's not just an expression—it can be the excuse for a really fun party for you and your friends.

Take a look in your closet and drawers. See that fuzzy black sweater that you *had* to have last season, but will never wear again? It may be just the thing that one of your friends is looking for. Chances are there's an old forgotten shirt in her drawer that you'd love to have, too. Bring your second-string wardrobes together for a clothes swap party where everyone arrives with clothes they don't want and leaves with stuff they love—all for free!

Here's how it works. Ask your friends to gather up and bag the clothes they won't wear anymore—things destined for the donation bin at your local charity store. The more friends you invite, the better the swap will be. Before the swap, make sure you have a full-length mirror on hand so your friends can try stuff on, and set up an area for a dressing room if you have the space. A bathroom will work just fine, or you can use a screen or curtain to section off an area of your room. Decide on an area to lay out the clothes. You can dump them all in a big pile on the bed or floor, or make it a big fashion event by giving friends hangers and letting them display the clothes around the room. Provide snacks and beverages for the swap—nothing major, just a few bottles of soda and chips or cookies are fine. Make sure everyone has a shopping bag for her found treasures (it's fun to decorate them, too—think of something cute like "Katie's Boutique," and make up your own logo).

There are some basic rules to follow for your clothes swap:

*Clothes must be clean and in relatively good shape.

*Don't "trade" one garment directly for another—give everyone a chance to see everything first and pick what they like.

*Expect a few minutes of chaos with everyone diving for things they want. Remember to be polite!

*If you see something at the same time as someone else, let her try it on. Try not to argue—it may not look good on you anyway.

*Keep your friends in mind as you look. Show them clothes that you think would look good on them.

*When you find something that you know you want, put it in your bag and move on.

*Don't forget that you can use clothes to make other things. You may not like the design of a particular item, but if you like the fabric you could use it to make something else, such as a purse or pillow cover. Think creatively.

*Share stories about your clothes! Friends will love to hear things like where you bought the item, what you wore it with, how much you liked it before it got too small.

*To make the party even more fun, have a fashion show, letting everyone show off their new items.

*At the end of the night, take all the leftovers that nobody wanted and put them in a big bag to drop off at a local shelter or charity store. Your parents will get a receipt for donation to use as a tax deduction. Now you've done something good for you and your friends, and also shared with people who really need the clothes!

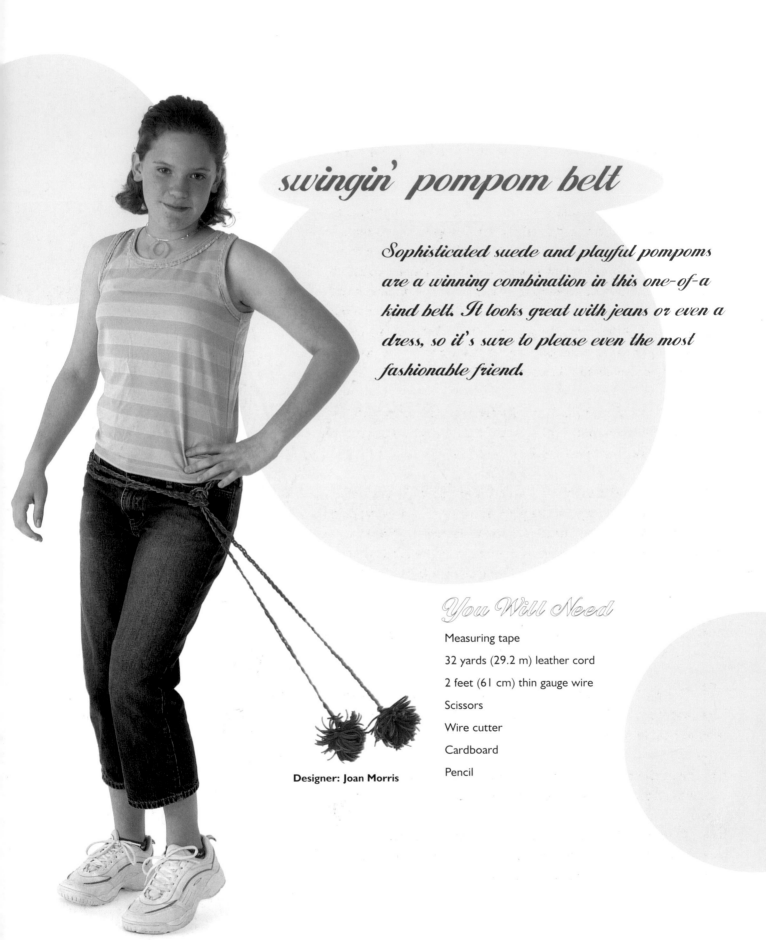

swingin' pompom belt

Sophisticated suede and playful pompoms are a winning combination in this one-of-a kind belt. It looks great with jeans or even a dress, so it's sure to please even the most fashionable friend.

Designer: Joan Morris

You Will Need

Measuring tape

32 yards (29.2 m) leather cord

2 feet (61 cm) thin gauge wire

Scissors

Wire cutter

Cardboard

Pencil

1. Measure and cut three pieces of leather cord, each 4 yards (3.6 m) long.

2. Lay the cords on a table side by side. At one end, measure down 6 inches (15 cm) and tie all the cords together in a knot. Start braiding the cords, as you would braid your hair, right after the knot. When braiding long lengths like these, it helps to attach the end to a doorknob to keep the tension even. Continue braiding the cords together until you get to 6 inches (15 cm) from the opposite end of the cords. Tie another knot. This should give you enough length to wrap the belt around twice and let the pompoms hang down about 18 inches (45.7 cm).

3. Draw two 5-inch (12.7 cm) diameter circles on your cardboard and cut them out. In the center of each circle, draw and cut out a 1-inch (2.5 cm) wide circle.

4. Measure and cut two 10–yard (9 m) pieces of leather cord. Place the two cardboard circles you cut together. Start wrapping one of the pieces of leather cord around the edge of the circle and through the hole in the middle. Keep wrapping the cord around the circle until you reach the end. The center hole will be almost completely blocked with cord at this point.

5. Using very sharp scissors, cut the cord around the outside of the cardboard between the two circles.

6. Cut a 12-inch (30.5 cm) piece of wire and slide it between the cardboard circles. Wrap it tightly around twice and twist the end to hold in place.

7. Slide the cardboard circles off each side. Trim any pieces to make the pompom even. Repeat this with the other pompom.

8. At each end of the braided cord, attach one of the leather pompoms by wrapping the ends of the belt around the wire and tying a knot. This will also hide the wire.

artful cards

If you're like most crafty types, you've probably got a big box full of paper scraps sitting around somewhere. Put them to good use by making cards for your friends. The key to making these simple designs look great is colorful paper, the bolder the better.

Designer: Nicole Tuggle

Folded paper card

Paper scraps of varying size and color

Clear-drying glue

Small paintbrush

Pencil (optional)

Scissors

Craft knife (optional)

for the card with stripes:

1. Cut the scrap paper into strips of varying width. Use papers in several different colors.

2. Brush a thin layer of glue along the back side of one of the strips. Press it down onto the front of the card, removing any air bubbles. Allow to dry. Repeat this step for the remaining strips. Be sure to leave 1/4 inch (6 mm) of blank space between each strip.

3. Once the glue has dried, simply trim the paper strips flush with the edge of the card.

for the card with circles:

1. With a pencil, lightly sketch out five or six circles from paper of different colors. They don't need to be perfectly round.

2. Cut out the shapes. Draw another circle on top of each cut-out circle. Cut out the inside circle with scissors or a craft knife leaving a circle outline.

3. Brush a thin layer of glue along the back side of one of the paper outline shapes. Press the shape down onto the front of the card, removing any air bubbles. Allow to dry. Repeat this step for the remaining shapes. It's fine to have some of the shapes hang off the edge of the card. This adds to an interesting composition.

for the card with squares:

1. Cut squares from the paper scraps. They don't need to be perfectly square.

2. Brush a thin layer of glue along the back side of one of the paper squares. Press it down onto the front of the card, removing any air bubbles. Allow to dry. Repeat this step for the remaining squares.

Designer: Kathryn Temple

friends forever flower card

This sweet card is easy to make and sends a meaningful message to the best of friends. If you're really feeling creative, try making the handmade envelope, too.

You Will Need

Cardstock

Scissors

Pencil

Scraps of decorative paper

Vellum paper

Flat-backed marble*

Fine-tipped marker

Craft glue

2 buttons with frame-like rims (optional)

Needle and thread (optional)

Small photos of you and your friend (optional)

Piece of ribbon (optional)

Beads (optional)

*Available at craft stores

1. Cut an 8 ½ x 11-inch (21.6 x 27.9 cm) piece of cardstock in half. Fold the remaining piece in half.

2. Cut out stem and leaf shapes from your decorative scrap paper. Glue them down.

3. Cut out petal shapes from the vellum. An easy way to do this is to fold the vellum several times then cut, so that you have identical petals.

4. Make a mark above the stem to mark the center of the flower. Glue one tip of a vellum petal down to this spot. Continue gluing petals in this fashion until you have a full flower.

5. Trace the shape of the flat backed-marble onto the paper you are using for your flower's center. Cut this shape out along the inside edge of your tracing line. You want the paper to be a little bit smaller than the marble.

6. Write your message—friends forever or whatever else you want to say—on the paper circle you made in step 5. Write your message slightly smaller than you want it to appear because the marble will magnify the letters.

7. Smooth glue onto the back of the marble. Press the circle of paper onto the back of the marble. Smooth out any air or glue bubbles.

8. Glue the marble into the center of the flower. Allow to dry.

Variation

Cut a long rectangle of paper. Fold the paper into thirds. Fold the bottom flap up and fold the top flap down over it. Taper the top flap into an envelope-flap shape (like you see in the picture above). Run a few dots of glue along the sides of the envelope to hold them in place, but leave the top flap open.

Close the top flap and make a mark near the edge where you want the button closure to go. Sew a piece of thin ribbon onto the flap in this position, then sew a button on top of the ribbon.

With the flap closed, decide where the second button closure should go and sew a button in that position. Tie a few beads to the end of your ribbon, securing them with a knot. Wrap the ribbon from the flap around the second button closure to close the envelope. Cut pictures to fit inside the buttons and glue them in.

best memories

You may not remember what you got for your birthday last year, what you were wearing on the first day of school (even though it seemed really important at the time), or what grade you got on that test you were stressing about, but chances are you remember even the littlest details of the times you spent with your friends. The jokes you told, the secrets you shared, and even the silliest, most embarrassing things that happened to the two of you make the best memories. Help keep those memories strong by making your friend a project from this section of the book. Whether you create a picture frame, a journal, a box, or even a calendar, it will always be remembered and it will always be special because you made it yourself.

photos-a-go-go

Chances are you and your friends have tons of pictures and tons of photo albums on your shelves. Here's one that really stands out. With a handle and a cute fabric cover, it's perfect for bringing pictures in to school to share.

You Will Need

- Small photo album, about 6 x 7 inches (15.2 x 17.8 cm)
- Measuring tape
- Fabric of your choice
- Scissors
- Quilt batting*
- Ice pick or awl
- Spray adhesive
- Hot glue and glue gun
- Square of adhesive-backed felt

- 24 inch piece of $^1/_{16}$-inch (1.6 mm) cable**
- Ferrule and stop**
- Assortment of $^3/_4$-inch (1.9 cm) buttons
- Assortment of $^3/_4$-inch (1.9 cm) plastic beads
- Plastic flower beads
- Pliers

*Available at fabric stores
**Available at hardware stores

5. For each inside cover, cut a piece of the adhesive-backed felt to fit. Pull off the backing and press the felt in place, covering the edge of the fabric.

6. Find the holes in the spine through the fabric and run the ice pick through the fabric and batting to open up the holes. Run one end of the cable through one of the holes from the inside to the outside.

7. Place one of the buttons onto the cable and start placing the beads onto the cable in a pattern. Leave about five beads in the center of the cable so that it will be comfortable to hold. When you get to the length you want, run the other button onto the cable.

8. Run the end of the cable down through the other hole in the spine to the inside of the album. Pull it across the spine to meet the other end. At the point where they meet, place the ferrule, running one end from one direction and the other from the other direction. Tighten this by pulling each end tight, then squeeze the ferrule with the pliers until it holds the cable tight.

Designer: Joan Morris

1. Cut the fabric piece to fit the cover of the photo album and wrap around to the inside about 1 inch (2.5 cm) on the top edges and 3 inches (7.6 cm) on the sides. Cut out a piece of the batting to the same size.

2. Get an adult to help you poke two holes in the spine of the photo album with the ice pick or awl, each about ½ inch (1.3 cm) in from the edges.

3. Adhere the quilt batting to the outside of the album with the spray adhesive.

4. Place the fabric over the batting right side up and wrap it around to the inside of the album. Hot glue the fabric in place by running a line of glue about 2 inches (5.2 cm) at a time, and then pressing the fabric into it. It's best to use low temperature glue for safety.

Designer: Kathryn Temple

days to remember calendar

Make your friend a homemade calendar marked with reminders of special days past and yet to come. This gift is great for New Year's or even the start of the school year, since it can easily hang in a locker.

You Will Need

Cardstock

Single and three-hole hole punches

Scissors

Patterned paper

Letter and number stamps and stencils

Inkpads in different colors

Ruler

Pencil

Binder rings

Acrylic paints

1. Before you get started, it's important to plan your calendar. Remember that the back of one monthly page is going to be the picture page for the next month. Use a three-hole punch to punch through 13 pieces of cardstock. On the opposite side of the pages, punch a single hole, centered near the top edge. This is the hole from which the calendar hangs.

2. For the days on the calendar, cut 1-inch (2.5 cm) squares from the patterned paper. You'll need about 35 for each monthly page. Stamp or stencil the date in the upper right hand corner of each square before you glue it down. That way, if you mess one up, you can re-do it before you have gone to the trouble of gluing it down.

3. Use a ruler and a pencil to divide each monthly page into a grid with seven equal columns. Use your stamps or stencils to write out the days of the month across the top of each page. Start with Sunday in the first column. Use abbreviations if there isn't enough room to write out the whole word. If you like, stamp or stencil the days on a strip of paper in a different color, then glue it to the monthly page. This is also a good trick to use if you mess up when working on the month page directly.

4. Next, glue the date squares down in five rows of seven squares each according to your grid. If you're using an 8 $\frac{1}{2}$ x 11-inch (21.6 x 27.9 cm) piece of paper, you will be able to leave a $\frac{1}{8}$- to $\frac{1}{4}$-inch (3 to 6 mm) space between each square. Make sure to look at a calendar or date book to check what day of the week the month begins on. For now, make a really light pencil mark indicating which month the page represents. You can erase it later.

5. When you have done the monthly pages for the calendar, put them in order and connect them with binder rings—you'll see how the back of one page will be the picture page for the next month.

6. Now for the really fun part—decorating each month's picture page with a new design. Use your stencils or stamps to write out the name of the month. Think about using colors or images that represent that month. You may want to stamp in the dates of special days or events that you and your friend are excited about, such as birthdays, the last day of school, or the trip you're taking. Finally, close the calendar and decorate the front cover by stamping or stenciling the year and adding images of your choice.

bead-azzling journal

Designer: Kathryn Temple

A journal is the perfect place to record memories, thoughts, and feelings. Make your friend a journal as unique as she is. Start with fabric in a pattern you know she'll like. Add beads to the fabric to make it eye-catching and extra special.

You Will Need

Purchased journal

Fabric with cool design

Piece of chalk or chalk pen

Scissors

Measuring tape or ruler

Seed beads and other small beads

Beading needle

Beading thread

Craft glue or spray adhesive

Chip paintbrush

Cardstock

1. Decide what part of the fabric's design you want to use as the focal point on the cover.

2. Place the journal on the back of the fabric with the focal-point design centered on the cover.

3. Use a piece of chalk to trace around the edge of the journal.

4. Measure 1 inch (2.5 cm) out from this rectangle on the top, bottom, and right side. Cut along this line.

5. Cut out a second rectangle of equal dimensions for the back cover.

6. Cut out a strip of fabric as tall as the two rectangles and about 2 inches (5.2 cm) wide for the spine.

7. Use beading thread and a needle to sew beads along the outline of the focal-point shape.

8. Brush glue onto the front cover of the journal and along the inside edges of the beaded outline.

9. Line the fabric up along the spine of the journal. Press and smooth the fabric onto the journal and fold it around the edges of the journal.

10. Repeat for the back cover.

11. Glue a strip of fabric onto the spine and trim it so that it's even with the top and bottom edges of the journal.

12. Cut two pieces of cardstock for the end papers (inside covers) of the journal. The end papers will cover over the fabric that's tucked around the edges from the front cover. Glue them in place. If the journal has blank pages in the front and the back, you could glue those down to serve as end papers.

13. Squirt glue into the inside of the beaded outline. You may need to use a small paintbrush to work the glue into hard-to-reach corners. Glue seed beads inside the outline. Allow to dry.

Designer: Kathryn Temple

the sweetest picture frame

You don't have to be a skilled crafter to make this frame, but you do have to love candy! Ask your friend to help you eat a bunch of candy—specifically, candy wrapped in beautiful, colorful foil. Use the empty wrappers to cover a frame, insert a picture of the two of you, and give it to her to remind her of sweet times spent together.

You Will Need

Multicolored-foil candy wrappers

Picture frame

Small paintbrush

Glue

1. Eat lots of candy with your friends and save the wrappers. You'll often find interesting wrappers on imported chocolates.

2. Remove the glass and cardboard backing from the frame.

3. Brush glue onto a small section of the frame, including the inside and outside edges and the back edge of the frame.

4. Press a foil wrapper onto this glued section and wrap it around the edges.

5. Continue until you've covered the entire frame with foil wrappers. Allow it to dry.

"got the t-shirt" memory quilt

Designer: Joan Morris

Have you ever heard the expression, "Been there, done that, got the T-shirt"? You and your friends probably have a lot of T-shirts from events you've attended or teams you've played on together. When you don't want to wear them anymore, make them into a quilt to remind you of all the fun you had. This project takes a little extra effort, but your friend is worth it, isn't she? You'll need a sewing machine and you'll need to know how to use it! Otherwise, you can ask your mom or another skilled sewer to help.

You Will Need

16 T-shirts

Measuring tape

Scissors

Rotary cutter and mat (optional)

Straight pins

1 ½-yards (1.4 m) fleece

1 ½-yards (1.4 m) quilt batting

Sewing machine

2 packages satin blanket binding

Matching thread

Embroidery floss

Embroidery needle

1. Cut the front off of the T-shirts. It's easy to cut the T-shirts with a rotary cutter and mat, but if you don't have that, scissors will also work. When cutting the T-shirts, leave as much fabric as possible, since some T-shirts could be smaller than others. You want the T-shirts to be the same size when cut. For this quilt, the T-shirts were cut to 10 x 14 inches (25.4 x 35.6 cm). Four of the T-shirts were small, so they were cut to 10 x 10 inches (25.4 x 25.4 cm) and used in the same row going across. As long as the T-shirts are the same width, it's OK.

2. Lay the cut T-shirts in a pattern you like, making sure the smaller ones are in the same row horizontally. Place the T-shirts together so that like colors and designs are not touching.

3. Sew the shirts together one vertical row at a time. Do this by placing the bottom right shirt and the next one up next to each other with right sides up and pinning them together. Machine stitch these pieces together with a ½-inch (1.3 cm) seam allowance. Next, place the next one up right sides together with the previous one and pin and stitch. Repeat the process with the last one in the row, then repeat for all the vertical rows.

4. Pin the first row on the right to the second row and machine stitch them together with a ½-inch (1.3 cm) seam allowance. Repeat with the next two rows. Hint: When sewing the rows together, if it looks like the corners of the T-shirts are not going to meet, you can pull on the shirt that's shorter as you sew and this will make the corners meet. Every shirt has a different stretch.

5. Measure the sewn-together T-shirts, and cut out the fleece to this measurement. Cut a piece of the quilt batting to the same measurement.

6. Lay the cut piece of fleece on a flat surface. Lay the quilt batting on top of that. Lay the sewn T-shirts on top of that face up.

7. You have two choices at this point: you can baste all the way around the quilt edge, then sew the blanket binding in place, or just take the blanket binding and pin it in place around the edge. The fold is placed on the edge, and the opening goes to either side of the quilt edge.

8. Machine stitch the blanket binding in place as close as possible to the inside edge, making sure to catch both edges.

9. At the corners, just fold the binding around and make a dart that runs to the outside corner. You can come back later and stitch the fold in place.

10. At the point where you join the next piece of binding, just machine stitch a seam joining the two pieces, making sure the raw edges are on the inside. Hint: if you miss catching any of the binding, just sew back over that area. If your thread matches, it won't show.

11. At all the places where four T-shirts intersect, use the embroidery floss and needle, stitch back and forth from the front to the back to the front again and tie a knot. Cut off the extra floss leaving a $1/4$-inch (6 mm) "puff." This will hold your quilt together in the center.

Friendship Quilts

Nowadays, if your friend moves across the country, you can still call and e-mail her, or even go for a visit. But back in the time of the pioneers, families were often uprooted from their communities and never saw their friends again. Mail was slow and unreliable, and photography was a new invention, so the average family couldn't afford to get pictures taken. So how did friends remember those who had moved away? Before there was e-mail, text messaging, or IMing, there were friendship quilts.

"Signature" or friendship quilts came into style in the 1840s, around the time permanent ink was invented. A woman would write or stitch her name on a piece of fabric, often adding a line of poetry or an inspirational quote beneath it. Squares of fabric were collected from a number of friends who would then come together and sew the quilt together, making a beautiful and cherished keepsake for a friend who was about to venture into unknown territory. Living in a new place, possibly quite isolated from other people, the woman could take comfort in her friendship quilt, remembering all the friends back home who were thinking of her and wishing her well.

Make your own friendship quilt like the one described here, or an updated version like the one on page 74. You'll be taking part in a long tradition and creating something that will be cherished for years to come.

Designer: Kathryn Temple

you and me box

Put a present inside it, fill it with little things you know she'll like or special mementos that mean something only to the two of you: this box is for symbols of your friendship. To make it even more personal, make sure the two girls on the box look like the two of you!

You Will Need

Templates on page 141

Colored poster board

Pencil

Scissors

Craft glue

Cardstock and regular paper in different colors

Marker (optional)

Rhinestones or buttons (optional)

1. Trace the template on page 141 onto poster board and cut out. Fold the corners and flaps of the box where indicated by dashed lines.

2. Glue the flaps down on the inside of the box. Let it dry.

3. Use the templates of the two girls on page 141 or design your own girls to look like you and your friend. For the clothes, use colors that the two of you usually wear, and chose paper that matches your real hair color. You can use a marker to add facial features if you like, or glue rhinestones or beads in the hair for barrettes or on the necks as jewelry, or add buttons to the clothes as we did here.

4. Glue one girl on each "door" of the top of the box.

Friendship Time Capsule

Where will you and your friends be in five years? How about 10 years? Do you think you will remember how things are today after so much time has passed? Why not create a record of your life right now to make sure you don't forget? Making a time capsule is a fun project that will help you and your friends document the way things are for you right here, right now, so that your memories won't be lost over time.

First, choose a container for your time capsule. You can use anything from a plastic food container with a lid to a shoebox. If you're planning on storing your time capsule outside, use an airtight metal container.

Next, it's time to fill the box with items that represent you and your friends at this particular moment in time.

Each friend should make a list of favorites including such topics as favorite song, book, actor or actress, color, TV show, movie, food, place, etc. Sign and date your list so that when you open the time capsule, you'll all remember who wrote what.

Include pictures of yourselves, your rooms, your pets, and your families. Write a brief description of the subject on the back of each photo. A school or class photo is also a nice addition, so you'll remember everyone, not just your close friends. School schedules or copies of recent reports or papers you've written will also be interesting to look at a few years down the road.

Cut out magazine pictures of your favorite stars and fashions. You may even want to include a small accessory, like a pair of earrings that represents your current style.

It's a good idea to include ticket stubs from movies or events you've been to recently. Definitely include a copy of the local newspaper for the day to show the date and give the future you an idea of what was going on in the world, how much things cost, etc., at the time you made the capsule.

Write a letter to yourselves in the future saying what's on your mind right now. You want your time capsule to be a snapshot of your life at this moment, including your feelings and your thoughts. Give yourselves predictions about what your lives will be like at the time you open the capsule. It will be fun finding out if they come true!

With your friends, decide on a time to open the time capsule—from one year to five years from now, or anything in between. Finally, decide on a place to hide the time capsule, seal your container tightly, tape down the cover, and put it away, making sure you make a note somewhere to pinpoint its exact location.

sights and sounds of friendship

Designer: Therese de la Baton Rouge

Here's a great gift that's easy to make and comes from the heart. Find an inexpensive photo album and CD case and decorate them—a matching set looks great. Fill the album with pictures of you and your friend together, and make a CD with all your favorite songs on it. It's guaranteed to be something she'll keep forever.

CD case and photo album

Eyelet setting tools**

Eyelet charms*

Eyelets**

*Available at craft stores

**Available at fabric stores

1. Make holes in the photo album and CD holder with the hole punch that comes with your eyelet setting tools. Be sure the holes are the same diameter as your eyelets!

2. Place a charm over one of the holes you punched. Slip an eyelet in the hole to hold the charm.

3. Set the eyelet with your setting tools.

Sierra & Daniela

Friends for six years

We like to do the same things and we can share secrets.

Girl's Mix Party

Create some great new memories by holding a CD-mix party with your friends. Ask each friend to bring her favorite CDs, then spend some time deciding which songs will go on a CD you'll burn for everyone in the group. Play around with the order of the songs so that you have a mix of tempo that goes from fast to slow or hard to soft. It's fun to choose songs that fit into a theme, such as Summer Songs (songs about summer or popular during your summer vacation) or Girls Rule (songs sung by female singers or bands). Here are some ideas of songs to include on your mix CD:

We have fun together and I can trust her.

1. A song that reminds you of a certain event or period of time, such as the song that was on all the time last summer, or one they played at a school dance

2. A song with a color in the title

3. A song with the name of one of your friends in the lyrics

4. A song that you listen to when you're sad

5. Favorite song by a band with the word "The" in their name

6. A song with a question word in the title (who, what, when, where, why, or how)

7. The song you would use to introduce someone to your favorite band (not necessarily their best song)

8. A song that gets stuck in your head all day

9. A song with lyrics you've never been able to understand

10. A song that you all know every word to

11. A song with the name of your city, state, or country in the title

12. A song you can't help dancing to

13. A theme song for each of your friends

The most important thing about a friend: She's considerate about your feelings, will stick up for you, and will keep your secrets.

Designer: Joan Morris

confetti memory box

Confetti is used for celebrations, so it's a great material to use on this box that celebrates your friendship. Give it to your friend filled with mementos—ticket stubs, programs, pictures, and notes—to remind you of times you've shared together.

You Will Need

Cardboard box

Precut confetti

Hole punch and colored paper (optional)

Decoupage glue

Paintbrush

Clear acrylic spray

Letter stickers (optional)

1. If you don't have confetti, you can make it by using a hole punch. Stack three different colors of paper and just keep punching.

2. Arrange the confetti on your work surface in an even layer that's wide enough to cover the side of the box you're working on.

3. Paint the decoupage glue thickly on one side of the box. Tip the side of the box that you've painted with glue into the confetti on your work surface and knock the side of the box to remove any that didn't stick. If there are any blank spots, you can fill them by placing the confetti on the box by hand. Let dry. Repeat this process for each side of the box and the lid until they are all covered.

4. Paint a layer of decoupage glue over the whole box and let dry. This will coat and hold down any confetti that might come loose. Let dry.

5. Spray the whole box with clear acrylic spray. Let dry and repeat.

6. If you like, add letter stickers to the top to spell out "Best Friends Forever."

Best Times

What's better than making stuff for your friends? Making stuff with them! In this section of the book you'll find project and party ideas that bring you and your friends together for creative fun. Whether there are two of you or many more, you'll have a great time making accessories for yourselves and for your rooms using all kinds of cool and unexpected materials. When you're done, you'll have something new that you or a friend made by hand and, more importantly, a great memory of the time you spent together.

Swapping Spaces

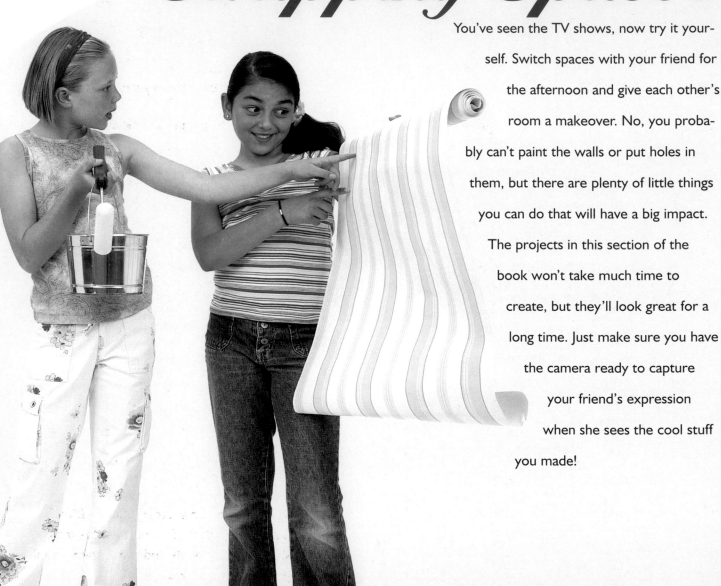

You've seen the TV shows, now try it yourself. Switch spaces with your friend for the afternoon and give each other's room a makeover. No, you probably can't paint the walls or put holes in them, but there are plenty of little things you can do that will have a big impact. The projects in this section of the book won't take much time to create, but they'll look great for a long time. Just make sure you have the camera ready to capture your friend's expression when she sees the cool stuff you made!

Friends for three years

She's funny and nice.

She's funny.

The most important thing about a friend: She's always there for you, she isn't mean, she's fun to be with, and she forgives you if you make a mistake.

Designer: Sonya Nimri

rose garden hatbox

This is a bouquet of roses that will last forever. The inside of the box is just as beautiful as the outside, making it a perfect place to store special things like letters, pictures, or a journal.

1. Cut the silk flower heads at the base and hot glue them onto the top of the hatbox with your glue gun, making sure there are no spaces showing between the petals.

2. Cut the leaves off the stems of the roses at the base. Put the lid on the box and hot glue the leaves to the sides of the box in an overlapping pattern like fish scales. Make sure not to glue any leaves under the lid of the box or the box won't close. *Really*, don't do it.

3. Lift off the lid and paint the part of the box that the lid covers and the inside of the lid green.

4. Hold one piece of ribbon inside the box, starting at the top and going to the bottom with just a little overlap on the bottom. Cut this piece and use it as a template to cut the rest of the ribbons that will line the inside of the box. Depending on the size of the box and the width of your ribbon, you'll probably need at least 20, but you may need to cut more later.

5. Spread some fabric glue on the back of the first piece of ribbon, avoiding getting sticky gluey fingerprints on the front side. Press the ribbon into place inside the box, starting from the bottom (just a little bit of the ribbon should be in the bottom of the box—you'll cover over the rest later) and moving upward, smoothing out any wrinkles as you go. When you get to the top of each piece of ribbon, fold it under and glue it to the inside of the box. Don't fold it over the top of the box because the lid won't fit over it. It's a pain to undo if you do it wrong, so pay attention.

6. Cover your cardboard circle in red fabric, gluing the excess tightly to the back. Glue the piece covered-side up to the bottom of the box.

7. If you like, glue garden catalogue pictures of roses to the underside of the lid, then brush a thin layer of decoupage glue over the top to keep them from curling up.

You Will Need

Hatbox or other round box

20 red and pink silk roses

Sharp scissors or wire cutters

Hot glue gun and glue sticks

Green paint

Paintbrush

About 3 spools of red and pink satin and grosgrain ribbon

Fabric glue

Red fabric

Cardboard circle measured to fit the inside of the box

Garden catalog pictures of roses (optional)

Decoupage glue (optional)

Paintbrush (optional)

watercolors jewelry box

Designer: Sonya Nimri

If this jewelry box were a painting, it would be a beautiful impressionist watercolor. You don't have to be Monet to make it, though. Instead of using paint, you'll use tissue paper as your palette and decoupage glue on your paintbrush. Your friend will cherish it as much as any masterpiece.

You Will Need

Wooden box or paper-covered cigar box

Tissue paper in different colors

Decoupage glue

2 sponge brushes, 1-inch (2.5 cm) size

Silk flower

4 round wooden knobs, flat on one side with a hole in the middle

Scissors

Hot glue gun and glue sticks

Piece of cardboard a little smaller than the inside bottom of the box

Quilt batting*

Piece of silk or other luxurious fabric

Craft knife

Satin ribbon

*Available at craft stores

1. Hold several layers of tissue paper together, and cut them into flower shapes.

2. Paint a thin layer of decoupage glue on your box, then place the tissue flowers on one at a time. Put flowers of the same colors in the same area to create a solid section of color. Start with lighter colors such as yellow or pink because lighter colors don't stain the brush. Blues and purples can leave a lot of color of the brush so use a separate brush for them so that your colors don't get all mixed up.

3. Brush another layer of decoupage glue on top of the tissue flowers, then continue to add more flowers on top of the first layer. It takes about six or seven layers of paper to properly cover a section. When you finish with one color, gradually start adding flowers of another color next to it and build up that layer too. As you're working, make sure not to decoupage between the crack of the lid and the box because this will prevent the box from closing. Decoupage the box with the lid shut so that the patterns spill over onto the sides.

4. When your box is covered to your liking, take your wooden knobs and use the same technique on them, but don't cover the flat side with paper. Hot glue the knobs to the bottom of your box near the edges to serve as feet for the box.

5. Glue the silk flower to the middle front of the box near the top so that it looks like a clasp if there is none.

6. When the box is completely dry, cut open the lid with the craft knife (you may need an adult to help you) and color the inside edges of the lid with a marker to match the paper.

For the inside of the box

7. Decoupage the inside sides of the box the same way you did the lid and the outer sides. Stop at the bottom corners of the box, extending just a little bit onto the bottom.

8. Cut a piece of cardboard to fit the inside bottom of your box with a little room to spare so that you can get the fabric around it.

9. Cut a piece of silk fabric about $1/2$ inch (1.3 cm) wider than the piece of cardboard on all sides. Wrap one side of the fabric around one side of the cardboard and hot glue it in place.

10. Cut a piece of batting to the exact size of your cardboard. Place the batting on the top side of the cardboard, then stretch the fabric over the batting, tuck it around the sides of the cardboard, and hot glue it in place.

11. Zigzag hot glue on the inside bottom of the box and glue the fabric-covered cardboard piece in place, padded side up, pressing the other side into the glue.

12. With the lid of the box open, hold up a piece of ribbon to stretch from the top of the main part of the box onto the lid. Add a little extra to the length, then cut one piece of ribbon for each side of the box. Hot glue one side of the ribbon to the main part of the box and the other end to the inside of the lid so that there's a little slack. The ribbon should stretch out straight with the lid open. Repeat for the other side of the box.

Designer: Therese de la Baton Rouge

love your lampshade

A lampshade is a perfect way to add a little personality to a room without spending a lot. Here are two great ideas your friend is sure to love. Best of all, both projects can be completed in under an hour.

You Will Need

Lampshade

Paper napkins

Scissors

Decoupage medium

Foam brush

Decorative fringe

Hot glue and glue gun

1. Cut out the designs on your paper napkins. You don't need to cut them out perfectly, so don't fret about it. Cut out lots of shapes.

2. The napkins are made of two or more layers of paper. Peel off the back layer of a shape you've cut out. Set the shape to the side. Peel off the remaining shapes. If you tear a shape, don't throw it away. Trim the torn edge and save the shape.

3. Brush a thin coat of decoupage medium on a small area of the shade.

4. Gently place one of your shapes on the shade. Use your brush to gently smooth the napkin onto the shade.

5. Cover the shade with shapes and let it dry.

Varation

Use the same fringe, with the balls cut off, for the top of the lamp shade.

Focus on Friends

Cierra & Leila

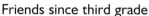

Friends since third grade

She's funny and fun to be with.

She's fun to be with and we like the same things.

The most important thing in a friendship: Honesty

back in time clock

Designer: Joan Morris

Take a trip back in time with this retro clock based on a design popular in the '50s. It's so cool that it never goes out of style. A clock this fantastic requires a little extra work, so ask a parent or other skilled person to help with the drilling and sawing.

You Will Need

4 wooden dowels, each 3 feet x ¼ inch (91.4 cm x 6.4 mm)*

Marker

Tape measure

Hand saw

Round wooden clock form, 7 inches (17.8 cm) in diameter*

Drill with ¼-inch (6 mm) bit

Super-strong craft glue

Clock kit (with longest center clock piece)*

12 wooden balls (predrilled doll heads), each about 1 ½ inches (3.8 cm) in diameter*

Craft paint in assorted colors

Clear polyurethane spray

Silver spray paint

Paintbrush

*Available at craft stores

1. Measure and mark your dowels in 10-inch (25.4 cm) lengths. Have an adult cut them with the hand saw. Keep the leftover dowel pieces for later.

2. On the edge of the wooden clock face, mark 12 spots corresponding to where the hour numbers would go. Be sure to line them up evenly, using the tape measure to make sure they are the same distance apart.

3. Ask an adult to drill ½ inch (1.3 cm) into the clock at each of the 12 spots you marked. To make sure you've drilled in far enough, mark that distance on the drill bit with masking tape, and always stop at that point.

4. Place a dab of glue on one end of each cut dowel and slide the dowel into the drilled holes. Make sure you push each dowel in all the way so each one will extend to the same point.

5. After the glue has dried, spray paint the clock face and dowels with the silver spray paint, front and back. Let dry and spray another coat.

6. Place the wooden balls on the ends of your leftover dowel pieces to help hold the balls in place while you paint them. Spray paint each ball a different color, using two coats on each if necessary. Let dry. Spray the painted balls with the two coats of clear polyurethane. Let dry.

7. Following the manufacturer's instructions, place the clock mechanism onto the clock face from the back and put the clock hands in place on the front. Don't forget the batteries.

8. Place a dab of glue on the ends of the dowels, and slide the balls in place. Let dry. Set the clock to the correct time.

marquee letter initial

If your friend has always wanted to see her name in big letters up on a movie marquee, here's a place to start. You can make her initial with papier-mâché—or use a premade initial from a craft store. If you make your own initial, get an adult to help you cut through the heavy cardboard.

Designer: Therese de la Baton Rouge

You Will Need

Corrugated cardboard from boxes or premade initial

Pencil

Metal-edge ruler

Craft knife

Masking tape

Newspaper

Clean, dry stones (optional)

White glue

Small bowl

Plastic trash bag

Brown wrapping paper (optional)

White acrylic paint

Decorative scissors

Colorful tissue paper

Sponge brush

Decoupage medium

Self-adhesive picture hanger (optional)

1. Decide how large an initial you wish to make. Ours is about 17 inches (43 cm) tall.

2. Use your ruler to measure and mark a square or rectangle on the cardboard. Sketch a simple block letter inside the area you marked using a ruler and a pencil to make the lines straight.

3. Get an adult to help you with this next step. Hold a craft knife against the metal-edge ruler and cut out the letter along the line. Don't try to cut through the cardboard in one pass. Make several cuts, holding your knife against the ruler as you cut.

4. After you've cut out the letter, trace around it onto another piece of cardboard. Cut out the second letter for the backside of the initial.

5. Measure and mark strips of cardboard 1 to 2 inches wide (2.5 to 5.1 cm). The strips can be as long as you like. Cut out the strips with your craft knife.

6. Giving the letter a shape is like making a box: you'll need to make sides for it. Hold a cardboard strip against one letter, mark the length, and trim the strip. Tape the strip into place with masking tape, then tape the back piece to the strip. The first few strips are a little tricky, but once you start adding more strips the letter will be more stable. Mark and trim another strip and tape it to the sides of the letter. Continue marking, cutting and taping strips to the letter. Leave the top or bottom of the letter open until last.

7. If you're going to stand the letter up, drop a few clean stones into the bottom. Crumple up newspaper and stuff it in the letter to hold the stones in place. If you are planning on hanging the letter, just stuff the letter shape with newspaper.

8. Close the last side of the letter with a cardboard strip taped into place.

9. Tear newspapers or brown wrapping paper into strips about 1 inch (2.5 cm) wide. Tear a lot of strips now before your hands get covered with icky glue!

10. Spread out a trash bag on your work surface.

11. Pour some white glue into a bowl. Paint all the surfaces of your letter with the glue and let it dry. If you're in a hurry, use a hairdryer to speed the drying process.

12. Pour white glue into a bowl and add almost the same amount of water. Stir up the glue.

13. Pick up one strip of paper at a time, dip it in the bowl, and then let the excess drip off the strip back into the bowl. You can also wipe off excess glue by pulling the strip between two fingers held together.

14. One at a time, place strips on your letter. Allow the strips to overlap as you place them. Once you have your letter covered, let it dry.

15. Cover your letter with one more layer of paper strips. Let it dry.

16. Paint the letter with the white acrylic paint.

17. Fold your tissue paper into layers. Cut out squares or other shapes with the decorative scissors.

18. Brush the decoupage medium onto a small area of the letter. Lay single pieces of tissue on the wet area, overlapping them just a bit. Use your brush to smooth the tissue to the cardboard. Cover your letter with tissue paper in the design of you choice.

19. Attach a self-adhesive picture hanger to the back of the letter if you wish to hang it on the wall.

Designer: Therese de la Baton Rouge

lovely to look at mirror frame

Does your friend spend a lot of time at the mirror, checking her look before going out in the morning? If so, she's sure to appreciate a beautiful mirror frame. Pick a piece of tissue paper with a pattern you think your friend will like, then pick another piece in a coordinating solid color. Decoupage them to the mirror frame for a new look in no time.

You Will Need

Flat-faced frame

Patterned tissue paper

Solid tissue paper

Decorative edge scissors

Decoupage medium

Foam brush

Craft knife or sharp scissors

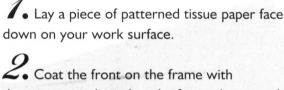

1. Lay a piece of patterned tissue paper face down on your work surface.

2. Coat the front on the frame with decoupage medium. Lay the frame down on the tissue. Turn the frame over and pat out the wrinkles with your foam brush. Let the tissue dry.

3. Coat one side edge of the frame. Wrap tissue around the edge to the back.

4. Adhere the tissue to the edge and back with medium. Work on one side at a time around the frame. Smooth the tissue with the frame brush as you go.

5. Lay the frame face down on your work surface. Use a craft knife or scissors to cut an X-shape in tissue in the center opening of the frame.

6. Coat the frame opening edges with medium and fold the paper around the edges to the back.

7. Cut strips of solid paper with your decorative-edge scissors. Glue them to the frame.

8. Insert a mirror (or a photo) in the frame.

Designer: Joan Morris

cast-off cardigan pillows

You may not want to wear your dear old cardigan anymore, but that doesn't mean you have to throw it away. While it may not look as good as it once did, it will probably look just fabulous on your friend's bed as a pillow.

Cardigan sweater (button or zipper-front)

16-inch (40.6 cm) pillow form*

Matching thread

Straight pins

Scissors

Sewing machine with zigzag attachment

*Available at fabric stores

1. Turn the sweater inside out. Slide the pillow form inside and center it in the best position to show the front of the sweater. Be sure there is enough room at the neck to stitch it together.

2. Pin the front of the sweater to the back of the sweater with the pillow in place. Pin as close to the edge of the pillow as you can without pinning it. At the corners, place the pins crossing over each other at the point of the corner.

3. Unbutton the sweater and remove the pillow form, keeping the sweater inside out.

4. Machine stitch a straight line all the way around on the pin line, removing the pins as you go. If you are using a zipper-front sweater, you need to stitch with caution over the zipper so you don't break the needle. It's also helpful to do a large zigzag stitch over the zipper to hold it in place. If your sweater has beads or pearls, stitch carefully over these areas, too.

5. Stitch a large zigzag stitch right outside the first line all the way around the pillow form.

6. Now stitch a straight line next to the zigzag line all the way around the pillow form. All these lines of stitching will keep the knit of the sweater from unraveling.

7. Cut around the whole sweater about ¹/₂ inch (1.3 cm) from the last stitch line.

8. Turn sweater right side out and stuff it with the pillow form. Button or zip it shut.

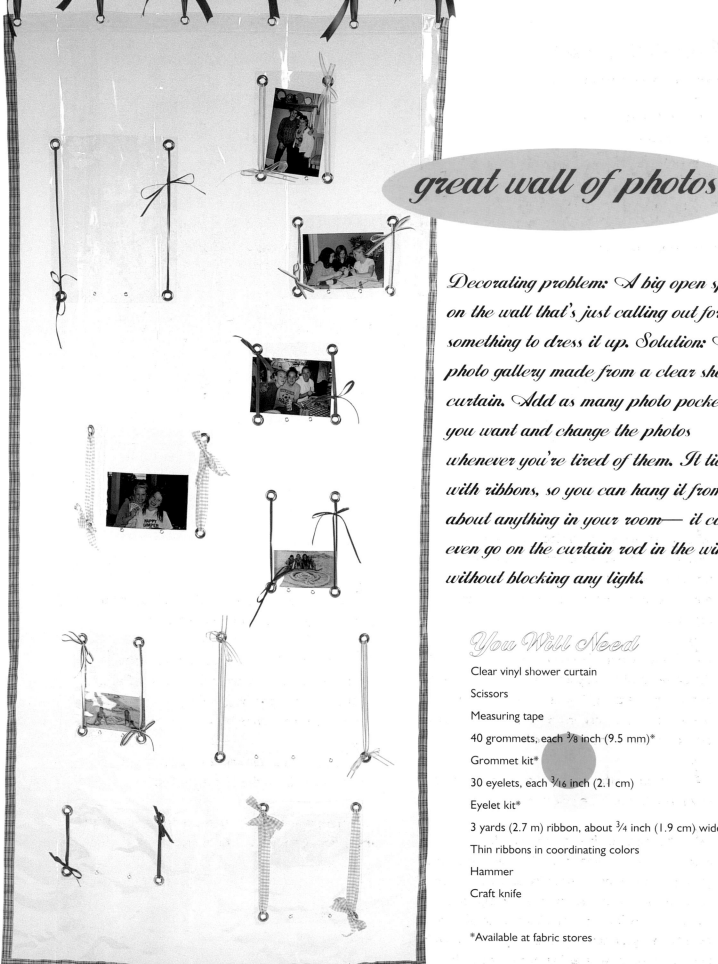

great wall of photos

Decorating problem: A big open space on the wall that's just calling out for something to dress it up. Solution: A big photo gallery made from a clear shower curtain. Add as many photo pockets as you want and change the photos whenever you're tired of them. It ties with ribbons, so you can hang it from just about anything in your room— it could even go on the curtain rod in the window without blocking any light.

You Will Need

Clear vinyl shower curtain

Scissors

Measuring tape

40 grommets, each ³⁄₈ inch (9.5 mm)*

Grommet kit*

30 eyelets, each ³⁄₁₆ inch (2.1 cm)

Eyelet kit*

3 yards (2.7 m) ribbon, about ¾ inch (1.9 cm) wide

Thin ribbons in coordinating colors

Hammer

Craft knife

*Available at fabric stores

Designer: Joan Morris

1. Cut the shower curtain to 32 inches (81 cm) wide.

2. With the leftover vinyl, cut out pockets in different sizes. Decide what size pictures you want to use and add 2 inches (5.2 cm) to each edge to have room for the grommets. For example, for a 4 x 6-inch (10.2 x 15.2 cm) picture, you'll need to cut a 6 x 8-inch (15.2 x 20.3 cm) pocket. A 5 x 7-inch (12.7 x 17.8 cm) picture would need a 7 x 9-inch (17.8 x 22.9 cm) pocket, and so on.

3. Place the pockets on top of the curtain in an arrangement you like. Follow the manufacturer's instructions for using the grommet kit to attach the pockets to the shower curtain. Make sure you attach the grommets close to the edges of the pockets so that the photos will fit inside without bending. At the bottom of each pocket, attach a few eyelets, according to the manufacturer's instructions. This will keep the photos from falling out of the bottom of the pocket.

4. Cut the ¾-inch (1.9 cm) ribbon into 18-inch (45.7 cm) lengths for the ties at the top of the shower curtain. Thread the ribbon through the grommets (these are the ones that were already in the shower curtain when you bought it). Tie the ends of the ribbon in a knot so that you have about a 3-inch (7.6 cm) loop.

5. On each pocket, tie thin ribbons through the grommets and eyelets in the design of your choice.

6. Place your favorite photos in the pockets and hang the photo gallery from the ribbon loops on top.

chan-deluxe light cover

Designer: Joan Morris

Hang it over a boring light fixture or anywhere else in the room. No matter where you put it, this fantastic fixture will be the center of attention. It's easy to make, but there's one catch: you'll need an adult to help you drill the holes in the hoops.

105

You Will Need

2 round wooden embroidery hoops (interior piece only), each 10 inches (25.4 cm) in diameter*

Measuring tape or ruler

Pencil

Drill and drill bit

Silver spray paint

Small chain, about 9 inches (23 cm) long**

Pliers

Binder rings in different sizes***

A few boxes of Christmas balls in different colors

*Available in craft stores
**Available at hardware stores
***Available at office supply stores

1. On the inside of each hoop, make four equidistant spots. Get an adult to help you drill holes at these positions. These are the holes through which you'll run the chain to hang the chandelier.

2. In between the holes you drilled in step 1, mark and drill additional holes. These are the holes from which you'll hang the Christmas balls. For this chandelier, we drilled three holes between each of the chain holes.

3. In a well-ventilated place, spray paint both hoops silver, and let dry.

4. Measure four pieces of chain, each 9 inches (23 cm) long. Use the pliers to open one link at the end of each 9-inch (23 cm) length, and slide the next section of chain off the previous one.

5. Insert the open link at the end of each piece into one of the holes you drilled in step 1. Use the pliers to squeeze the link shut over the wood.

6. Attach the other end open of each piece of chain to the corresponding hole in the second hoop and close the link the same way you did in step 5.

7. Using the same technique you used in step 4, cut three lengths of chain, each 16 inches (40.6 cm) long. Cut one length 20 inches (51 cm).

8. Attach each of the lengths of chain you cut in step 7 to the top link of the chains on the top hoop. Close with pliers.

9. Use the pliers to attach the shorter three lengths of chain to the long one 4 inches (10.2 cm) down from the end. Fold over the end of the long piece to create a loop at the top, and attach it in the same way with the pliers.

10. Divide the balls into two groups of equal size—half for the top ring and half for the bottom. Attach the hangers of the balls to the binder rings. You can make the clusters different sizes by adding binder rings in various sizes.

11. Attach the binder rings to the hoops through the holes drilled earlier. Keep playing around with them until you get the look you want.

Designer: Therese de la Baton Rouge

paisley crazy desk organizer

There may be a way you can help your friend with her homework even if you're not there while she's doing it: create a fun desk organizer that will make the time she spends at her desk more pleasant. This project is really easy to make and is sure to be appreciated.

Unfinished wooden box or CD holder

Paintbrush

Acrylic paint

Pencil

Paisley template on page 140

Tissue paper

Stapler

Decorative-edge scissors

Decorative hole punches

Foam brush

Decoupage medium

1. Paint the wooden box with one coat of acrylic paint and let it dry for an hour or two. Give the box a second coat of paint and let it dry overnight.

2. Photocopy the paisley template on page 140.

3. Lay the paisley template on a folded piece of tissue paper and trace around the shape with a pencil.

4. Staple the folded tissue around the outer edge of the shape you traced. This will help keep the tissue layers together as you cut out the shape.

5. Cut out the shape with decorative-edge scissors. Keep the stack of tissue together as you make the last cut.

6. Use the hole punches to make decorative patterns in the paisley shape.

7. Use a large hole punch to punch out some larger shapes (flowers, dots, or any other shape).

8. Spread a coat of decoupage medium on a small area of the box.

9. Lay one tissue paisley on the box. Use your foam brush to pat the shape into place. Gently brush the shape to remove any big air bubbles or wrinkles. Be careful, the wet tissue will tear easily!

10. Cover the surface of the box with tissue-paper paisleys. Allow the box to dry overnight.

11. Give the box a final coat of decoupage medium to seal it.

Craft Night Party

In the old days, women got together and made quilts, gossiping and laughing as they sewed. Everyone pitched in, and when they were finished they not only had a great quilt, but they had passed many enjoyable hours with their friends.

You and your friends may not know how to quilt, but you can still have a great time making things together. Pick a craft material, any craft material. Buttons, flat-back marbles, even old magazines. Whatever you choose, get a super-size supply. Invite your friends over and spend the afternoon or evening using what you've got to make jewelry, hair accessories, or whatever else your brilliant minds come up with.

Instead of a quilting bee, it's a button bee, a marble bee—well you get the picture! The projects in this section of the book provide you with inspiration—the rest is up to you!

Lindsey & Kelly

Friends for six years

She's fun and lifts your spirits.

She can keep secrets, we get along well, and she is there for me.

The most important thing about a friend: Friends should keep your secrets, be there for you, and be funny.

Button Bowl Projects

Buttons are a great craft supply that you can find in large quantities at craft stores, fabric stores, or even flea markets or antique stores. They're usually pretty inexpensive and come in an amazing variety of colors, textures, and styles. For a fun craft night party, pour a big collection of buttons into a bowl and try one of the following projects. Depending on which project you pick, you'll need to provide a few more inexpensive materials. To get started, you can pour the contents of the bowl onto the table or floor and watch everyone pounce on the buttons they want to use. It's fun to see all the different designs your friends come up with using more or less the same materials.

blooming buttons t-shirt

Designer: Joan Morris

Such a great idea, so easy to do. Even if you've never sewn in your life, you can sew a button on a shirt, and this project will give you plenty of practice. By the time you're finished you'll be a pro!

T-shirt for each girl

Assorted buttons*

Colored dressmaker's pen* (you can use a regular pen if you're careful to cover the mark with a button)

Matching thread

Sewing needles

Scissors

*Available at fabric stores

1. Separate the buttons into piles of similar colors: greens for the stems and leaves, pinks and oranges for the flower.

2. Lay the shirt flat on a table, front side up. Arrange the buttons on the shirt in a design you like.

3. Use the dressmaker's pen to mark where each button is going to be sewn on. One by one, pick up each button and mark its position. You may want to lay the buttons down on the table or a piece of cardboard in the design shape, so you don't forget what went where.

4. It's best to start sewing at the top of the shirt so that as you're sewing you're not working over sewn-on buttons. Thread the needle with the matching color and knot the end, doubling the thread.

5. From the front of the shirt, run the needle through to the back and back to the front. This keeps the knots away from the inside of the shirt and hides them under the button. Slip the button onto the thread and onto the shirt. Run the needle through another hole in the button to the inside of the shirt, and then back up through the first hole to the front. If you have a 4-hole button, just stitch a cross in the center. Do this three or four times for each button to be sure the button will stay on through washing.

6. From the inside of the shirt, push the needle through the shirt so it comes out under the button. Cut the needle off, leaving enough thread to tie a knot. Tie a knot (it should be hidden under the button) and trim the ends.

7. Repeat the process until you have sewn on all the buttons. To wash the shirt, turn it inside out. This will protect the buttons and it will be a lot quieter in the dryer.

button jewels necklace

Designer: Kathryn Temple

A button-filled choker necklace is a great accessory to have, and since each of your friends will pick different buttons and create her own designs, everyone will leave the party with a fabulous piece of jewelry.

You Will Need

Assorted buttons

Thin black elastic

Scissors

Necklace closures, 1 hook and 1 loop per necklace*

*Available at craft stores

1. Think about a design for your necklace. If you have a variety of buttons in different sizes, you may want to stack small ones on top of larger ones for a different look. Think about which colors of buttons will look good next to each other. Experiment with different combinations until you get a look you like.

2. Cut a piece of elastic to fit your neck, taking the stretch of the elastic into consideration. Hold the piece of elastic around your neck to see what fits, then add a little more to that measurement to accommodate the knots you'll be creating. Once you've got the correct measurement, cut the elastic.

3. Attach one end of the elastic cord to the hook necklace closure and knot it several times to make sure it's secure. Add your first button by threading the cord through the first hole in a button twice for a secure bond to the neck closure. Then thread it through the next hole in the button, starting from the underside.

4. Attach your next button to the cord and thread the cord through the first, then the second hole in the button. Continue adding buttons to the cord in this manner. If you want to add a small button on top of a larger one, simply place the small button on top of the large one with the holes aligned before you thread the cord through.

5. When you get to the end of your cord, thread the cord through the last hole of the last button twice, then make a knot. You should have enough cord left to knot the thread around the loop closure several times, creating a knot each time. If you haven't left enough cord, just take off the last button and use your second-to-last button as the last one. Cut the excess cord after you've knotted the cord securely to the loop closure.

top button earrings

Substitute buttons for beads to make eye-catching earrings in a snap. Buttons in different shapes and sizes make for an interesting design. If dangly earrings don't work for you, just stop after you've added the first or second button for a close-to-the-ear look.

You Will Need

Tiger-tail jewelry wire*

Wire cutters

Assortment of buttons

Needle-nose pliers

Crimp beads*

Earring findings (2 for each pair of earrings you want to make)*

*Available at beading or craft stores

1. Cut a long piece of wire with your wire cutters.

2. Run a piece of wire from under your first button, up through one of the holes, back down through the second hole and behind the button.

3. Add a second button to the wire and repeat the process, but this time run the thread over the button and into the first hole, then under the button and back out the second hole. For this design, a small button was stacked on top of a larger one, but the design is up to you.

4. Take the wire emerging from under the second button and thread another button onto it, running the wire over the top of the button, into the first hole, under the button, and out the second hole. Now send the wire back through the first hole and back under the button. Add a crimp bead to the wire with the needle-nose pliers.

6. Thread the wire back under the next button, through the first available hole, over the button, then down through the remaining hole and back under the button. Add a crimp bead to the wire.

7. Thread the wire over the button, through the first hole, under the button, then back out the remaining hole, and under the button. Twist your wire back onto itself, leaving a small loop at the top, and add a crimp bead.

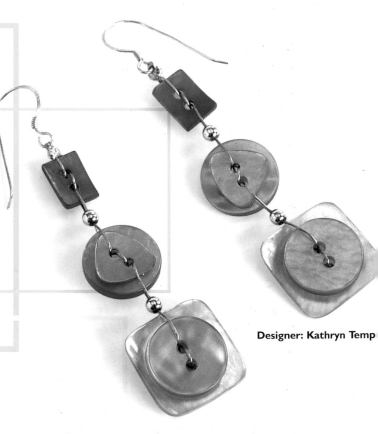

Designer: Kathryn Temp

8. Slip the wire loop through the loop at the bottom of the earring finding. Repeat the process for the second earring in the pair.

Button Cookies-in-a-Jar

For your button crafts party, how about serving button cookies? Here's a fun recipe that everyone can help make. Or as a special party treat, give each friend a jar full of ingredients that she can take home to bake.

¾ cup (150 g) granulated sugar
1 cup (200 g) oatmeal
1 cup (200 g) chocolate candy
¾ cup (150 g) brown sugar, firmly packed
2 cups (400 g) all-purpose flour
1 teaspoon (5 g) baking powder
½ teaspoon (2.5 g) baking soda
Crispy rice cereal
Funnel
Wide-mouthed jar
1 egg
1 stick of butter
Spoon

Assembling the Ingredients
In the given order, layer the ingredients in a 1-quart (1 L) wide-mouth jar, using a canning funnel. Pack each layer very firmly.

Baking Instructions
Place the contents of the jar into a bowl. Add 1 egg and 1 stick (½ cup [115 g]) butter or margarine. Mix well with a spoon. Drop by the spoonful onto a lightly greased cookie sheet. Bake at 350°F (176°C) for 10 to 12 minutes.

Friends for six years

She's nice, funny, and kind.

She's funny and adventurous.

The most important thing in a friendship: Friends should stand up for each other, like the same things, and be adventurous together.

Marble Mania

Flat-backed marbles were invented for use in floral displays, but crafty girls everywhere realized that these inexpensive little gems had a multitude of uses for other craft projects. Gather a bunch of them together in a box—they come in a variety of sizes and colors—and invite your friends over for an evening of marble mania. Here are three great project ideas to get your creativity started.

too cool for school belt

Designer: Joan Morris

Binder rings usually hold your papers together at school, but for this belt they can hold together a stylish outfit. Pick magazine images with a theme—for this belt we used illustrations of girls' faces—and attach them to the flat back of marbles. The rest of the process is just as easy, and the result is a creative accessory.

1. Cut out images in 1½-inch (3.8 cm) squares—you can trim them later.

2. Lay the pictures flat face up.

3. On the flat side of the marbles, brush on a thin layer of decoupage glue and place it glue side down over the image. You can move it into position for a few seconds before the paper rips.

4. Once the marbles are dry, you can cut the pictures to shape by holding the scissors close to the marble and sliding the marble around as you cut.

5. Place the marble on the synthetic suede and draw around it. Cut just inside the circle you drew so that the synthetic suede circle is a little smaller than the marble.

6. Attach the synthetic suede to the back of the marble with the super-strong glue. Let dry.

7. Place a bolo-tie slide between two binder rings, sliding each ring under one of the hooks and squeezing them shut with the pliers. Don't squeeze too tightly though— you want the rings to be able to slide. Repeat this process with all 12 rings and bolo slides. At one end, leave the ring open. At the other end, place a bolo-tie slide on the ring and the swivel hook on the other. It's best to keep all the ring binder hinges facing in one direction.

8. To make sure the ring binders don't open, place a dab of industrial glue on the opening with a toothpick. Also place a dab of glue where the swivel hook attaches to the bolo-tie slide.

9. To attach the marbles to the bolo-tie slides, place a layer of industrial glue on the bolo-tie slide and place the flat side of the marble in position. Let dry. You can make the belt shorter or longer by simply removing or adding binder rings and bolo tie slides.

You Will Need

Images from magazine

Clear flat-back marbles, each about 1 inch (2.5 cm) in diameter*

Scissors

Small paintbrush

Decoupage glue

12 binder rings

12 bolo-tie slides*

2-inch (5.2 cm) swivel hook

Synthetic suede or felt scraps*

Pliers

Super-strong craft glue

Measuring tape

Toothpicks

Pen

*Available at craft stores

marble art hair accessories

Another inventive use for flat-backed marbles. Use this idea to make hair accessories that match any outfit. The materials are so inexpensive you can make a different one for every day of the week!

You Will Need

Images from magazines

Scissors

Clear flat-back marbles, each about 1 inch (2.5 cm) in diameter*

Small paintbrush

Decoupage glue

Super-strong craft glue

Clear headband, hairclip, or barrette

Designer: Joan Morris

1. Cut out images or patterns from magazines and lay them face up. Place marbles on top of the images to determine what part of the picture fits the marble's size. When you have a design you like, cut out the pictures with about 1/2 inch (1.3 cm) extra all the way around. You can trim the picture later to fit exactly.

2. On the flat side of the marbles, brush on a thin layer of decoupage glue. Place the glued side down over the image. You can move it into position for a few seconds before the paper rips.

3. Once the marbles are dry, you can cut the pictures to shape by holding the scissors close to the marble and sliding the marble around as you cut.

4. Arrange the marbles in a design you like and use the super-strong glue to attach them to the hair accessories.

flower power mirror

Designer: Joan Morris

You Will Need

Large round mirror and several small round mirrors*

Pencil

Frozen-treat stick

Quick-drying epoxy**

Nail polish remover (optional)

Flat-back decorative marbles in a variety of colors

Sawtooth hanger

*Available at craft stores

**Available at craft or hardware stores

Here's a cute and simple idea for a mirror makeover. Using flat-back marbles in a variety of colors and inexpensive mirrors in two sizes, create flower shapes within flower shapes or come up with your own design ideas. This is a no-skills-necessary project that everyone can enjoy.

1. Place the small mirrors in a circle face down on a flat surface. The edges of each mirror should touch the others.

2. Center the large mirror face down on top of the small mirrors. Arrange the mirrors until they make a flower shape. Use a pencil to draw around the edge of big mirror, creating an outline of the mirror on the back of the small mirrors.

3. Pick up the large mirror and put it aside. One at a time, pull up each small mirror and dab epoxy onto the area inside the pencil line using the frozen-treat stick. Don't put on too much epoxy because it can ooze out onto the large mirror. Once you've got epoxy on the back of each small mirror, place the large mirror on top of them face down.

4. Check the manufacturer's instructions to find out the dry time for the epoxy. When it's dry and the small mirrors are affixed to the large one, pick up the large mirror and turn it over. If any epoxy oozed out on to the large mirror, it can usually be removed with nail polish remover.

5. Start arranging the flat-back marbles on the small mirrors in flowers shapes. Choose different colored marbles for the "petals" and the flower centers.

6. Glue the marbles in place one at a time with the epoxy. Let dry.

7. Turn the large mirror over and place the saw tooth hanger on the upper center of the large mirror and use the epoxy to adhere it in place. Let dry.

Focus on Friends

Emily & Mary Ann

Friends for six years

She's someone you can really trust.

She's funny, nice, and is the life of the party.

Friends should always stand up for you and be there for you.

Spa Party

Pamper your friends with a spa party where you sip fruit smoothies and make soap, lotion, and scrubs that smell divine and make you feel fantastic. Making your own bath and beauty products is so much more fun than buying them, and doing it with friends is a perfect party activity. Poll your friends in advance to find out their favorite scents so you can buy essential or fragrance oils they'll like. Assemble the materials you need, using the recipes here as a guide. The ingredients are all natural, so they're safe to use, but make sure you have an adult on hand to help with the microwave—hot wax can splatter! Check with your friends to find out if they have any allergies to the oils you'll be using or any other components of the recipes. Make sure you have lots of containers and embellishments—decorating the containers is half the fun of making the projects!

lavender hand and body lotion

Designer: Allison Smith

This lotion smells yummy and feels light and soothing on your skin. If you're making this project with a lot of friends, don't forget to adapt the recipe to make enough lotion for the whole group—this recipe makes just enough for one container of lotion. If you'd like to make another project too, make some extra so you can create the scrub on page 124. Make sure you have enough containers and plenty of stickers, markers, buttons, or other embellishments so that each friend can decorate her own label.

You Will Need

Measuring cups or spoons

1/2-cup (118 ml) grape seed oil*

2 tablespoons grated beeswax*

Large glass measuring cup

Spoons

Microwave

1/4-cup (60 ml) witch hazel*

1/4-cup (60 ml) orange water*

1/2-teaspoon (2.5 g) borax**

Blender

Lavender essential oil*

Lavender soap color***

Small clear plastic bottle

Stickers or blank labels for embellishment

*Available at health food stores

**Available at drugstores

***Available at craft stores

1. Combine the grape seed oil and grated beeswax in a large glass measuring cup. Get an adult to help you microwave it for 30 seconds and then check to see if the oil and beeswax have melted. If not, continue to melt and check every 20 seconds until everything is melted together.

2. Combine the orange water, witch hazel, and borax in a blender and pulse until the borax is dissolved.

3. With the blender running, slowly drizzle the oil mixture into the orange water mix.

4. Continue blending until the cream becomes light and fluffy, but don't over blend.

5. Set aside ¼ cup (60 ml) of the lotion for the Honey Almond Exfoliating Scrub on page 124.

6. Add a few drops of lavender essential oil and lavender soap color to the lotion and stir gently to combine.

7. Pour the lotion into a bottle and decorate the container as you like.

Spa Night Smoothie

A girl can work up quite an appetite making all those wholesome, healthy beauty supplies. Treat your friends to some delicious smoothies while they work. Make sure you label the smoothie mixture, though. You'll be using the blender to make beauty products, too, and this smoothie looks an awful lot like the lavender lotion. It tastes a lot better, though!

You Will Need
½ pint (200 g) blueberries
¾ cup (250 g) plain-low fat yogurt
¼ cup (60 ml) milk
¾ teaspoon (8 g) vanilla extract
Blender
1 tablespoon (12 g) honey (optional)

Put all the ingredients into a blender and blend until smooth. Taste the smoothie after it's blended. If it's not sweet enough, add the honey.

honey almond exfoliating face scrub

Designer: Allison Smith

If you made extra lavender lotion from the recipe on page 122, use it to make a great-smelling exfoliating scrub that will leave your face fresh and flake-free.

You Will Need

Measuring cups and spoons

¼ cup (60 ml) of leftover lotion from the lavender lotion recipe (page 122)

2 tablespoons (50 g) grated opaque glycerin soap*

2 tablespoons (50 g) ground apricot kernels**

1 tablespoon (25 ml) honey

Several drops almond essential or fragrance oil**

Small, round plastic or glass container

*Available at craft stores or online soapmaking suppliers

**Available at health food stores

1. Place the grated soap in a glass measuring cup. Get an adult to help you melt the soap in the microwave until it's liquid but not boiling. Microwave it at 50 percent power for 30 seconds, and then check it every 20 seconds to make sure that it isn't boiling.

2. Add the remaining ingredients and stir until combined.

3. When the mixture has cooled a bit, place it in a small container and decorate the container.

moisture wand lotion sticks

Designer: Allison Smith

Wave your magic wand and make dry skin disappear. These cute roll-up lotion sticks are petite and portable, the perfect item to stick in your purse and break out after a long day at school makes your skin feel parched.

You Will Need

Measuring cups or spoons

¼ cup (50 g) grated beeswax, loosely packed*

¼ cup (50 g) grated or flaked cocoa butter, loosely packed*

¼ cup (50 g) shea butter**

1 tablespoon (14.7 ml) coconut oil**

1 teaspoon (5 ml) lanolin**

5 lotion tubes*

*Available at craft stores or online cosmetic supply sources

**Available at health food stores

Note: This recipe makes enough for five lotion sticks. Double, triple, or even quadruple it depending on how many you need for your party.

1. Place all the ingredients in a glass measuring cup.

2. Get an adult to help you heat the mixture in the microwave for 30-second intervals until all the ingredients have completely melted.

3. Get an adult to help you pour the lotion into the lotion tubes or a soap mold.

4. Allow the lotion to cool, and then embellish the containers.

say it with flowers soap

Designer: Allison Smith

Here's a fresh soap design that's always in season. For the flowers, choose scents and colors that you and your friends will like. You'll need to have an adult help you melt the soap in a microwave, but shaping your soap flowers is all up to you.

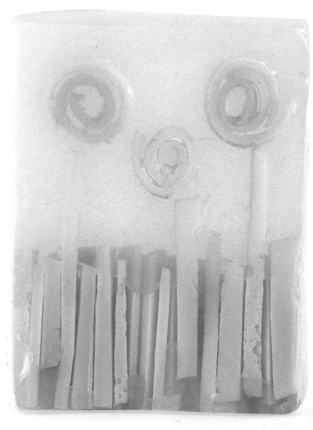

You Will Need

½-cup (57 g) opaque glycerin soap*

Knife

Microwave

Clear glass measuring cup

Spoons

Toothpicks

Soap scents*

Soap color*

Bar-shaped soap molds*

Vegetable spray

Vegetable peeler

Clear glycerin soap*

Alcohol in a spray bottle**

Clear plastic wrap

*Available at craft stores or online soapmaking supply sources

**Available at drugstores

1. Chop ¼ cup (35.5 g) of the opaque soap into ½-inch (1.3 cm) cubes.

2. Place the soap cubes in a glass measuring cup. Melt the soap in the microwave until it's liquid but not boiling. Microwave at 50 percent power for 30 seconds, and then check every 20 seconds to make sure that it isn't boiling.

3. Add pale green color and stir well.

4. Spray the mold lightly with vegetable spray.

5. Pour the soap into the mold.

6. Repeat the process with the rest of the opaque soap, adding the color you choose for the flowers to the second batch.

7. Allow the soap to harden completely before unmolding.

8. Slice the green soap into small matchstick-sized pieces.

9. Use the vegetable peeler to make small curls out of the colored soap for the flowers.

10. Spray the mold with vegetable spray.

11. Arrange the colored soap into flower-and-stem designs. Spritz the pieces with alcohol.

12. Chop ½ cup (57 g) of the clear soap into ½-inch (1.3 cm) cubes.

13. Get an adult to help you with this next part, since you'll be dealing with boiling hot liquid. Place the soap cubes in a glass measuring cup. Melt the soap in the microwave until it's liquid but not boiling. Microwave at 50 percent power for 30 seconds, and then check every 20 seconds to make sure that it isn't boiling.

14. Allow the soap to cool for a few minutes, then gently pour the clear soap over the flower designs, being careful not to mess up the design.

15. Allow the soap to harden completely before unmolding. Wrap it in clear plastic to store it.

Designer: Kathryn Temple

spa slippers

Ask your friends to come to your spa party with their ordinary slippers. With a little creativity, some felt, and other materials, they'll leave with special spa slippers that are perfect for pampered feet.

You Will Need

Marker

Felt squares in different colors

Scissors

Buttons

Needle and thread

Pin findings*

Strong fabric glue (optional)

*Available at fabric stores

1. Draw a petal shape onto the felt with your marker. Experiment with different flower petal shapes—long, thin ones look like daisies or sunflowers; shorter rounded ones could be roses, pansies, or violets. Make different shaped petals on different colors of felt. Once you've gotten the shape you like, cut it out to use as a template for the rest of the flower petals.

2. Fold the base (the thinnest part) of the first petal into a "w" shape and sew through the layers with the needle and thread.

3. Continue with the same thread and add more petals in the same way.

4. When you have added enough petals, sew through the first one and pull the petals into a circle.

5. Make a knot and sew a button, a circle of felt, or some combination of these things into the center of your flower.

6. Sew or glue the flower onto a pin finding.

Two of a Kind

You don't need a big crowd around to have a good time. Try these projects, which are meant to be made by an awesome twosome. Matching bags, pendants, and a make-it-together lamp are tailor-made for a dynamic duo, two peas in a pod, two of a kind friends… well, you get the picture—your best friend and you.

Focus on Friends

Olivia, Alex & Jasmine

For a long time!

Jasmine is sweet, Alex is funny.

Olivia is funny and nice.

The most important thing in a friendship:
Trust, sense of humor, caring, and loyalty.

cut from the same cloth purses

Designer: Kathryn Temple

The saying "cut from the same cloth" means two people are just alike. These purses are cut from the same cloth, namely an old pair of pants. Each purse is made from the bottom of one leg. This a great project for two friends who are cut from the same cloth to try together.

You Will Need

Pair of pants, preferably in a velvety fabric

Measuring tape

Scissors

Ribbon in coordinating color

Needle and matching thread

Thin elastic cord

Buttons

Beads of your choice

18-gauge or stronger wire

Needle-nose pliers

1. Cut off the bottoms of the pants about 9 inches (23 cm) from the hem.

2. Turn the pants inside out and sew along the bottom seam.

3. Keeping the pants inside out, flatten each of the bottom corners to make a "T" with the bottom seam. Sew these corners flat. They should be about 2 inches (5.2 cm) wide.

4. Turn the purse right-side out and sew 6-inch (15.2 cm) pieces of ribbon to the inside edges to serve as handles.

5. Cut a 4-inch (10.2 cm) piece of thin elastic. Fold it in half and tie a knot in the end, forming a loop.

6. On the middle inside edge of one side of the purse, sew the knot of your elastic loop securely to the purse.

7. On the outside of the other side of the purse, sew a button in the top center.

8. Use the needle-nose pliers to make a loop on the end of a 4-inch (10.2 cm) piece of thick wire. String a variety of beads on the wire and make a loop at the other end. Connect the end of the wire to the elastic loop inside the purse and close the wire loop with the needle-nose pliers.

9. Fasten the purse closed by pulling the elastic loop around the button.

birds of a feather purse

If you and your friend are birds of a feather, why not make matching feather-edged purses? These are inexpensive and easy to make, not to mention lots of fun to carry.

You Will Need

Feather boa, 6 feet (1.8 m) long

Canvas tote, about 8 inches (20.3 cm) in diameter

Needle and matching thread

Straight pins

Scissors

1. Find the center thread of the boa. This is what you need to stitch around to hold the boa to the tote. Pin the boa to the top edge of the tote bag.

2. Run the threaded needle (with the end knotted) through the tote, around the center thread of the boa, and back through the tote. When you pull the thread around the boa, try to catch as few of the feathers as you can. Keep stitching about 1/2-inch (1.3 cm) apart all the way around. When you've completely circled the top of the tote, you can either cut the boa off at this point (be sure the boa won't unravel, most won't) or you can start stitching it around one more time to give the feathers a fuller look.

Designer: Joan Morris

hand-and-hand pendants

In the past, friends used to exchange locks of each other's hair as tokens of friendship. Update the tradition with these hand-print pendant charms. Each one is as unique as your individual hand prints. Make sure an adult helps you bake the poylmer clay in the oven.

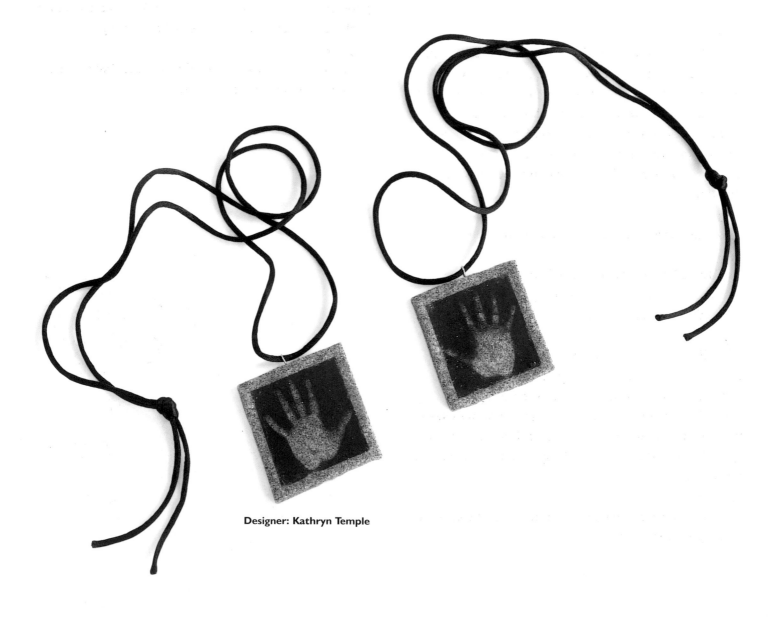

Designer: Kathryn Temple

Photocopies of you and your friend's hands

Scissors

Polymer clay

Oven

Needle-nose pliers

Silver wire or paper clips

Black cord or ribbon

1. Make photocopies of your hands by placing your palms flat against the glass of a copy machine. Use the "reduce" keys on the copier so that the copies of your hands are much smaller than real life. The hands in these charms were reduced to 25 percent of life-size. Make two copies of each—you want your hand-print on one side of the pendant and your friend's on the other.

2. Cut out a square shape around each hand.

3. Knead the clay until it's soft. Press it out into two flat pieces that are about $1/8$–inch (3 mm) thick and wider than the hand copies.

4. Press each of the copies FACE-DOWN onto the polymer clay. Make sure that you keep track of which end is up. You will not be able to see through the copy once it's pressed down, and you need to know where to attach the silver loop. Use the back of a spoon to smooth down the copies, making sure that there are no air bubbles.

5. Cut around each copy so there is a $1/8$-inch edge (3 mm) around the copy.

6. Cut two pieces of wire, each about 1 inch (2.5 cm) long. If you are using paper clips, straighten them out with your needle-nose pliers first.

7. Use the pliers to make a loop at the end of each of the wire pieces.

8. Carefully push the straight end of the wire into the top edge of the polymer clay squares.

9. Bake the pendants according to the manufacturer's instructions.

10. After letting the pendants cool, peel off the photocopies. If they do not peel off easily, run them under cool water and rub off the paper with your finger.

11. Run a piece of cord through the silver loop on each pendant and knot the ends.

Designer: Kathryn Temple

put your hands together lamp

When you were little, you probably did hand-print art, but this project takes it to a whole new level. Ask your friend to give you a hand making a funky lamp out of little more than some tissue paper, a recycled bottle, and some inexpensive minilights.

You Will Need

Office paper and pencil

Scissors

A clear glass bottle such as an empty juice bottle

Multicolored tissue paper

Decoupage medium or glue

Sponge brush

Short strand of minilights

1. You and your friend will both need to trace around your hand onto a piece of paper, then cut out the hand print. Use the hand print as a template to cut out the same shape from colored tissue paper.

2. Brush the surface of the bottle with glue.

3. Cover the whole surface of the lamp with a light-colored piece of tissue paper. Brush the decoupage medium or glue over the tissue paper.

4. Press your hand shapes onto either side of the bottle and brush over them with decoupage medium or glue.

5. Cut different shapes out of tissue paper and add them to the lamp in the design of your choice, brushing over them with decoupage medium. Let dry.

6. Feed a string of lights into the bottle, leaving the plug end and a little bit of the wire coming out of the opening of the bottle.

templates

Henna Stencil Clothes, pages 44-46

Paisley Crazy Desk Organizer, page 107

You and Me Box, page 77

Acknowledgments

This book was a lot of fun to make thanks to a lot of talented people. All the designers (see the list below) who made the projects you see in the book were a joy to work with—thanks to each of them for their time, energy, and creativity. Our models (listed below), photographer Sandi Stambaugh, and stylist Jarita Wright helped create all the great photography in the book—great job everyone! Thanks to art director Tom Metcalf for his styling, cool design, and all the effort and enthusiasm he brought to the project, and to August Hoerr for the beautiful illustrations. Thanks to Kelly Robinson for her expert proofing, and Paige Gilchrist, Nathalie Mornu, Amanda Wheeler, Meghan McGuire for editorial assistance of all types.

Our Models

Sierra B.

Pearl C.

Calleigh C.

Autumn D.

Skyla D.

Daniela D.

Olivia H.

Kelly J.

Alex L.

Emily L.

Cierra M.

Lindsey O.

Amber P.

Natasha P.

Niroshka P.

Candace R.

Kate R.

Leila S.

Ginny S.

Mary Ann S.

Jasmine V.

Contributing Designers

Therese de la Baton Rouge is an all-around craft maven who has contributed to many Lark Books including *Girls' World (Lark, 2002)*. She is especially fond of using vintage and Indian-inspired patterns and colors in her work.

Joan Morris is also an all-around craft maven, talented at sewing, jewelry making, and making fashion accessories of all kinds. When she's not running her coffee shop, she's often found at home, entertaining or making fabulous things with her charming dog, Zoe.

Sonya Nimri, aka the Dumpster Diva, loves making one-of-a-kind fashion and home accessories. You can see more of her work at www.dumpsterdiva.com.

Emma Pearson makes children's clothing and hats, and much, much more. Her work has appeared in many Lark books, including *Gifts for Baby (Lark, 2003)* and *The Artful Cupcake (Lark, 2004)*.

Allison Smith is the author of *The Girls' World Book of Bath and Beauty (Lark, 2004)*. She loves concocting all-natural beauty products in her kitchen and sharing them with her daughters and friends.

Kathryn Temple teaches art to elementary and middle school kids when she's not working in her painting studio or making things for Lark Books, including *Paper Fantastic (2004)* and *Cool Jewelry (2005)*.

Nicole Tuggle specializes in handmade books and cards. You can see more of her work at www.sigilation.com.

Index